No Sidewalks Here

A Pictorial History of Hillsborough, California

MICHAEL SVANEVIK

SHIRLEY BURGETT

CUSTOM & LIMITED EDITIONS
San Francisco

Published by Custom & Limited Editions
San Francisco, California

Designed by Morris Jackson

Second Edition

Library of Congress Cataloging-in-Publication Data:

Svanevik, Michael, 1942–
        No sidewalks here : a pictorial history of Hillsborough,
California / Michael Svanevik, Shirley Burgett.
        p.   cm.
    Includes index.
    ISBN 1-881529-36-3
    1. Hillsborough (Calif.) — History — Pictorial works.   2.
Hillsborough (Calif.) — Biography — Pictorial works.   I. Burgett,
Shirley.   II. Title.
    F869.H64 S83 1999
    979.4'69—dc21   99-21199
                                                                    CIP

Printed in Spain D.L.TO: 767-1999

This book is dedicated to the generous spirit
of the citizens of Hillsborough, past and present,
who created, built and have maintained
this unique community.

The publication of
No Sidewalks Here
is sponsored by

Proceeds from the sale of this book benefit Hillsborough City Schools

Introduction

April 25, 1910. A special election for the incorporation of a new town. Hillsborough, an exclusive enclave for the millionaire elite.

St. Matthew's Military School, set on an 80 acre expanse in the heart of the proposed town, was designated as the polling place. Clubman Francis Carolan arrived in an ornate two-seated carriage driven by a finely liveried footman. His team of thoroughbred bays was adorned with gold-mounted harnesses.

C. Templeton Crocker, impeccably dressed grandson of the transcontinental railroad builder, a candidate for membership on the new town's board of trustees, sped up in an imported German automobile.

Lumber millionaire George A. Pope reached the polling place in his chauffeur-driven French limousine with cream colored upholstery and trimmings.

Gray uniformed cadets of the military school passed smartly in review. A baseball game was played in the afternoon for the entertainment of voters.

Sixty cast ballots for incorporation. One voted against. Hillsborough, perhaps Northern California's most unique community, came into existence officially May 5, 1910. A democracy deluxe.

Hillsborough, California

Six square miles on the San Francisco Peninsula, nestled in the hills west of the County Road, 18 miles south of the city. It was bound by San Mateo, Burlingame and the Crystal Springs lakes.

This unique experiment in municipal democracy began in 1893 when a group of wealthy and influential San Franciscans, most a generation removed from their hard working pioneer parents, established the Burlingame Country Club.

The *Burlingame Club*, as it was commonly known, soon became a center of high society. San Francisco's fashionable set gravitated toward Burlingame to engage in English-style fox hunting, coaching, polo, beagling, golf, tennis and other invigorating activities to which the parvenu society thought it should become accustomed.

Life in Burlingame changed dramatically in the hours after the 1906 earthquake as many San Franciscans, formerly summer residents only, moved permanently to the Peninsula. Even before her house burned on the afternoon of April 18, 1906, Abby Parrott (widow of the Gold Rush banker), along with her family and servants, was moving to San Mateo.

Although wagons were at a premium in San Francisco on the day following the earthquake, Cecelia Casserly ordered her butler to go out and find one. A hearse was all that he found available. One infant son, Michael, made the trip down the Peninsula in a laundry basket on the floor of the hearse. The family stayed temporarily in San Mateo while their home on Bridge Road was under construction.

In the years after the earthquake, sounds of hammers and saws echoed through the wooded hills west of County Road as other great homes were built. William H. Crocker commissioned *New Place*. Not long thereafter, when his original home burned, financial titan Joseph D. Grant began *Villa Rose*. San Francisco *Chronicle* publisher George Cameron transformed a once humble cottage into majestic *Rosecourt* and civic leader George A. Newhall embarked on elegant *Newmar*. C. Templeton Crocker employed eccentric architect Willis Polk to design palatial *Uplands*. Never one to be outdone, Harriet Pullman Carolan, daughter of the Pullman palace car builder, along with her husband Frank, embarked on the most ambitious undertaking of them all, the 96-room *Carolands* chateau atop Black Mountain.

To the south was San Mateo, already a booming middle class community. Burlingame, where the middle class population mushroomed with the influx of earthquake refugees, was incorporated in 1908. The fashionable colony surrounding the country club viewed the rapid growth of neighboring communities with alarm, fearing that their exclusivity was threatened.

Hillsborough was incorporated in 1910 as an act of community self defense, a town for the financially privileged. Most were millionaires and proud of it. Wealth, many Americans still believed, was a sign of divine favor. It was to be protected and respected, never apologized for.

Their goal was a town of rustic simplicity—guaranteed by charter provision, a document which substantiated the town's claim of uniqueness. There were to be *no* businesses—*no* stores, boarding houses, tenements, hotels or gas stations; *no* telegraph or express office, *no* jail, *no* churches or other places of worship. And, to maintain the bucolic air, there were to be *no* sidewalks. Meetings of the town council, solons insisted upon calling it the *board of trustees*, were held in the evening. Perhaps appropriately, members costumed themselves in formal evening dress.

Hillsborough houses, many with a decidedly old world charm, were set on large grounds, usually secluded by brick walls and thick hedges to assure privacy, something apparently cherished in the town above all other things.

In early Hillsborough, there were two country clubs, and most people belonged to one if not both. The prestigious *Burlingame Club* was the first such institution in California. From the time of its incorporation in 1893, it became the virtual center of the community's social life and its membership the dominant force—both political and social—in the town.

Then there was the *San Mateo Polo Club*, with its fine playing field and elaborate clubhouse on El Cerrito Avenue. In the early years of the decade, polo, known as the *sport of kings*, became the town's passion and favorite pastime, avidly played by sons of the first families. El Cerrito field was the place to be and be seen. Polo jargon became an essential part of a Hillsborough lady's social equipment.

Until World War II, outsiders, and many town residents as well, habitually referred to Hillsborough as the *perfumed society*, a place where differences in social class were determined only by the size of the house, the number of servants and the number of automobiles a family owned. Most households had live-in servants. Children were raised by governesses or nurses; few ate at their parents' table until age 11 or 12. At 13 most boys were sent off to boarding schools. Girls spent an extra year or two at home.

The *Hillsborough lifestyle* was the delight of the local press. When fire broke out at night, the town's regular department invariably was assisted by high bred society folks in evening dress, the women often in costly gowns and wearing priceless gems. The San Francisco *Call* poked fun at the town in a thoroughly tongue-in-cheek editorial noting that in Hillsborough "each fireman will have an assistant, a private secretary and a valet to help with his gold-nozzled hose."

From its earliest years, town police noted license numbers of automobiles driven after dark. Residents were asked to call police about unidentified cars parked in their neighborhoods. During the late 1940s and early '50s, those seeking access to homes in the Carolands tract on Black Mountain were stopped by a guard at Ralston and Eucalyptus. Identifications were checked and their coming telephoned ahead. As late as the 1990s, police officers stopped strangers to politely inquire if drivers wanted assistance finding an address.

For all the fun that has been poked at Hillsborough, it has been the home of some of the state's most powerful and respected personalities. Banker William H. Crocker and neighbor William B. Bourn dominated Northern California water resources. They bank-rolled hydroelectricity in California, and along with Eugene de Sabla pioneered Pacific Gas & Electric Co.

Joseph D. Grant, who began his professional career in the dry goods firm of his Scots immigrant father Adam Grant, was one of the first in the West to recognize the potential of oil. Along with Hillsborough neighbor Capt. John Barneson, he formed General Petroleum, and well before World War I, they were operating a fleet of 14 tankers exporting oil to Argentina, Japan and China.

With the instincts of his canny father, Grant also joined other Hillsborough neighbors investing in and pioneering hydroelectricity. Recognizing the need for steel production in the West and believing such essential for the economic growth of the state, he established and was president of Columbia Steel Co. In 1908, he opened a foundry at the town of New York on Suisun Bay—a community soon renamed Pittsburg after the flourishing foundry in the East.

Parenthetically, Grant also was a founding member of the Burlingame Club and San Mateo Polo Club. He helped introduce the game of golf on the Peninsula and was one of the first to encourage development of polo. A multi-millionaire and eminently successful, Grant despised office work. He maintained a 12,000 acre ranch near Mount Hamilton, where he bred polo ponies.

More than any other single person, Hillsborough resident Henry T. Scott advertised the industrial potential of San Francisco Bay. As president of the Union Iron Works, he was the first Western builder of U.S. warships. After 1903, when he sold the iron works to Bethlehem Steel, he invested in Pacific Telephone and Telegraph Co., serving both as the company's president and board chairman. Scott, always a favorite of Hillsborough children, was mayor and spent several terms on the town board of trustees, until his retirement in 1926.

Cecelia Cudahy Casserly, daughter of the Chicago meat packing magnate, mother of four children and hostess of some of the most elaborate social affairs of the early century, worked for the Red Cross during World War I and later cast aside her brilliant gowns in favor of a severe, olive-drab Army uniform when she accepted the invitation of the Secretary of War to become "Director of Women's Relations for the Army," the most powerful woman in the service.

Casserly ran unsuccessfully for Congress, the only Hillsborough woman ever to be a congressional candidate. Determined to make the Bay Area a cultural center, she was a force behind creation of the Philharmonic Society of San Mateo County and, in the late 1920s, the construction of Woodland Theater adjacent to Hillsborough School. And all the while she continually shocked neighbors in the millionaire suburb through her vocal support of "equal pay for women performing the same duties as men" and "to help women gain the rights to which they are entitled."

In the generation before World War I, many wealthy Hillsborough families married their daughters to English and French nobility along with other well-placed Europeans. In part, it was for this reason that no California community was more avid in its support of the war. Hillsborough School children staged pageants and poloists played matches to raise funds. Many volunteered for military service; some were killed.

The William H. Crockers, William Bourns, Francis Carolans and John Casserlys were recipients of coveted French Legion of Honor awards, presented (1919) for support of France even before American military involvement. They engaged in fund raising, supported the Lafayette Escadrille, sent ambulances to the Western Front and participated in building and staffing the American Ambulance Hospital in Paris, that city's most modern hospital.

In 1918, after a victory parade of honking motor cars through the winding drives, Hillsborough life returned to normal. Population rose slowly. The prestige of the country club grew and some of the most important business matters in the history of the state were concluded in its lounges.

Most old-time town residents will agree that the big change in the life of the community came with the manpower shortages of the Second World War. Many Hillsborough residents joined the service and moved away.

Those who remained behind rallied to the colors. The country club became a recreation area for military men. The old Barneson estate was turned into a dormitory for Naval officers and *Newhall Manor* was taken over by Phyllis Tucker and the ladies of the American Women Voluntary Services. Throughout the war, that organization served dinners and provided entertainment to officers stationed nearby. At *Home Place*, the sprawling estate of Jennie Crocker Henderson, the swimming pool and pool house were practically turned over to armed forces personnel for their enjoyment.

At war's end, many families who had moved away returned. Most servants never did. Maintaining great estates was increasingly expensive and difficult. One after another they were sold and subdivided.

Though many descendants of the first families maintained Hillsborough homes, the town ceased to be the exclusive aristocratic municipality. Newcomers, servicemen and others, who had been introduced to the town during the war, now remained. By the end of the 1940s, Hillsborough had become the mecca of successful business professionals. Dentists and doctors—originally regarded by the founding elite as mere craftsmen (only one was admitted to the country club's early membership)—expanded the town's growing population.

For all the pride that early residents had in their ultra-exclusive community, they seldom called it Hillsborough. Most believed it sounded too pretentious. Those north of Barroilhet said they lived in Burlingame. Those further south called it San Mateo. One long-time resident declared, "we'd gag every time we said the word *Hillsborough*."

The town's traditional Anglo-European character underwent alteration in the 1960s with the arrival of the first Asian residents. Until then Asians had only been in Hillsborough as servants or in work gangs. Two decades later there came an influx of new immigrants (equally well-to-do as the town's pioneers) from Hong Kong, Taiwan and Singapore. By 1990 a third of the children in the municipality's four public schools were of Asian origin. Student bodies became increasingly diverse with the addition of Middle Easterners, Filipinos, Hispanics and African-Americans.

Hillsborough is still a well-to-do community. In more recent years, many town residents have devoted their energies to charitable works, notably for the Medical Mission Sisters, the Junior League, Stanford Children's Hospital, the San Francisco Symphony Auxiliary and the Coyote Point Museum.

Perhaps most notable is the *Concours d'Elegance*, created in 1956 by a group of Hillsborough mothers intent on raising money to augment meager school budgets. What started with a mere handful of parents putting on an automobile show has grown dramatically. By the 1990s, an army of more than a thousand people—accountants, doctors, teachers, attorneys and many other professionals—contributed time to make the effort successful. In 1991, the one-day event, along with tennis and golf tournaments, dinner dance and other fund raising activities, garnered more than a quarter of a million dollars for the town's public schools. This effort has made Hillsborough City Schools some of the finest in the state.

No Sidewalks Here: A Pictorial History of Hillsborough, California has been put together in part because no work of this magnitude has been undertaken before, and to record the existence of a unique community. Proceeds from the book's sale support Hillsborough's public schools.

The authors are regular historical columnists for the Peninsula *Independent*, a newspaper serving communities throughout San Mateo County. Through the use of anecdotes and photographs, the book presents a social history of Hillsborough. *No Sidewalks Here* doesn't pretend to be a complete story.

Most photographs used in the book have been lent by residents or former residents of the town. Locating them was something of a treasure hunt. Some, magnificent family treasures, were borrowed off of living room walls. One Hillsborough family located an antique trunk of photographs in an attic and invited the authors to study and copy its contents.

Other photographs were found in states outside of California. Probably the single most exciting discovery consisted of two leather bound albums crammed with photos, many of them quite small, of early Hillsborough which had been snapped by the family between 1890 and 1915. These were unearthed in Sun Valley, Idaho.

This has been a genuine community effort involving interviews with town and school officials, representatives of the police and fire departments and dozens of Hillsborough residents.

The text accompanying the photographs is true as far as can be determined. If an item used has been part of the oral tradition and couldn't be supported with documentary evidence, that has been noted.

Photographs are also true. That is, they have not been altered or "cleaned up" by a computer to make them appear more artistic. Scratches or tears in originals have been faithfully reproduced.

In both words and pictures, *No Sidewalks Here: A Pictorial History of Hillsborough, California* portrays a most distinctive town.

Michael Svanevik & Shirley Burgett
San Mateo, California
February 1999

No Sidewalks Here

George Howard

Howards of *El Cerrito*

The Howard residence called *El Cerrito* was considered the first large home in what became Hillsborough. Once thought to have been built early in the 1850s by landholder and San Francisco merchant William Davis Merry Howard, it is now believed the big house wasn't constructed until after his death in 1856. *El Cerrito's* true builder was Howard's younger brother George, who was executor of W.D.M. Howard's estate and who married his brother's attractive young widow, the former Agnes Poett. This photograph was taken in 1864 on the porch of the home (at the junction of De Sabla Road and Sherwood Court). In the generation after their marriage (1857), George and Agnes transformed what had been an ordinary residence into one of the showplaces of the Peninsula. George is standing (center); at left is William Henry Howard, Agnes' son by her first husband. She is not pictured.

John Parrott II

Carriage of John and Abby Parrott at Baywood

Of the early estates, none was grander than John Parrott's *Baywood*. The dapper Parrott, *beau brummel of the Peninsula gentry*, purchased Frederick Macondray's estate on San Mateo Creek in 1859. Most of the property was located in what became Hillsborough but was annexed by San Mateo during the 1920s. Parrott's carriages were absolutely regal, and he maintained a stable of the finest carriage and riding animals. In 1868 he replaced the old house with a sprawling gingerbread mansion called *Baywood* (on the south bank of San Mateo Creek, west of the County Road). U.S. Consul at Mazatlan during the 1840s and later a prominent San Francisco banker, Parrott was the most aristocratic of Peninsula patricians. He died in 1884, survived by a wife and nine children. Two daughters married French noblemen, Christian de Guigné and Auguste de la Lande. One married Scots soldier-aristocrat Archibald Douglas Dick. A son and one daughter married into the locally powerful Donohoe family (builders of Union Iron Works). Son John Parrott II (pictured), a founder of the Burlingame Country Club, is wearing the uniform of a U.S. Consul once worn by his father.

John Parrott

Oak Grove School

Prior to the arrival of San Francisco's perfumed society, which transformed it into large estates, the Hillsborough area was characterized by acres of grass punctuated by ancient oaks. This photograph, circa 1890, was taken on the 156-acre expanse comprising Oak Grove School, a private boarding institution for boys. School advertising touted *"natural beauty,"* promising an isolated environment where pupils would be free of *"boys who exert bad influences"* as well as *"the undesirable sway of the city."* Virtually self-sufficient, Oak Grove had its own vegetable gardens, orchard and dairy.

Before the advent of the Burlingame Country Club (1893), the region's proudest institution was Oak Grove School, a private educational lyceum for boys presided over by Ira D. Hoitt, *A.B.M.A.* Classes were held in the one-time residence of J.H. Redington, described as west of the Oak Grove Station and two and a half miles south of Millbrae, "the nearest village." The school's purpose was *"to stimulate in the boy manly impulses, quicken and strengthen his sense of duty and moral courage, contribute vigor to his physical development, lead him to a clear idea of right and to the acquisition of such mental furniture as shall prepare him for admission to the best college, university or technical school in the land or for a successful business life."* Enrollment was limited to 50 pupils.

Students at Oak Grove School

Hawaiian Princes, students at St. Matthew's Military School

Kip Hall, St. Matthew's Military School

For 49 years, St. Matthew's Military School was the county's most prestigious educational institution. Established (1866) by Episcopal minister Alfred Lee Brewer, it was a finishing school for boys offering strict discipline and first-rate education. Originally situated on Baldwin Avenue adjacent to St. Matthew's Episcopal Church, it moved (1892) to an 80 acre site on the upper end of Barroilhet Avenue, which became the Brewer Tract in Burlingame (later Hillsborough). Sons of the local elite as well as boys from all over the West attended. Three Hawaiian princes were schooled there. Stanford, the University of California and a dozen Eastern colleges accepted graduates without further examination. During its years of existence, there were only two headmasters: Alfred Lee Brewer and his son, the Rev. William Brewer. The younger Brewer became Hillsborough's first mayor. The school closed in 1915.

C. Templeton, Mary and Jennie Crocker

Col. Charles Frederick Crocker

Col. Charles Frederick Crocker (eldest son of transcontinental railroad builder Charles Crocker) married Jennie Mills Easton. The union resulted in three children but Mrs. Crocker died within days of the last birth. Crocker, though plagued by ill health, became associated with Southern Pacific and rose to vice president. Super patriotic, he was a life member of the California National Guard. Commissioned second-lieutenant, he was shortly transferred to the governor's staff as a lieutenant-colonel. He died of Bright's disease at 43 (1897). The three children— Mary, Charles Templeton, and Jennie—came under the care of their maternal grandmother. Upon reaching maturity, Mary moved East, where she died in an automobile accident. Templeton, elected to Hillsborough's first board of trustees, was the town's best known *bon vivant*. Jennie became one of Hillsborough's most popular women and lived until 1974.

Henry T. Scott and Adeline Mills Easton

In 1857 Gold Rush ship chandler and Burlingame pioneer Ansel Easton married Adeline Mills, sister of California banker and financier Darius Ogden Mills, for whom Millbrae is named. Their daughter, Jennie Mills Easton, went to the altar with Col. Charles Frederick Crocker. The three children of this marriage were orphaned in 1897. Their grandmother, Adeline Mills Easton, is pictured with industrialist Henry T. Scott in the gardens of the Crocker family home, *Montes Robles* (built in the 1870s by William Henry Howard and originally called Uplands). Henry Scott was both a family friend and Jennie Crocker's trustee.

Montes Robles, **originally called** *Uplands*

In 1892 Francis G. Newlands, son-in-law of the late William Sharon and executor of his estate, began developing Burlingame Park as a country enclave for well-to-do San Franciscans. California's original, hard working pioneers were now gone, and the city's high society was largely composed of the second generation idle rich, a group devoted to pleasure rather than toil. Newlands planned the West's first country club to create enthusiasm for his land development. The original clubhouse (1893) was in a cottage designed by A. Page Brown. The next year it was moved to a mansion built in the 1870s by Alfred Poett and more recently owned by lumber tycoon George A. Pope. Architect George H. Howard Jr., one of the club's founding members, was retained to design its third home (pictured). The white plastered building was occupied in 1899.

Burlingame Country Club orchestra, circa 1900

Burlingame Country Club designed by George H. Howard Jr.

During the club's early years the emphasis was on elegance. Originally servants and cooks were provided by the Palace Hotel in San Francisco. Guests arrived by train at Oak Grove station and were taken to the club by hotel coaches. Pictured is a turn of the century luncheon on the ivy-covered veranda of the gabled clubhouse.

Of all Burlingame-Hillsborough pioneers, none was more sensitive than intellectual Henry P. Bowie, who in 1879 married Agnes Poett Howard, widow of *both* W.D.M. Howard and his brother George. In 1886 Bowie began building *Severn Lodge* on West Santa Inez Avenue. Agnes died in 1893. That year Bowie sailed for Japan, where he fell under the spell of Nippon. He learned to read, write and speak the language while studying Japanese painting and poetry. Back in Burlingame in 1904 to complete *Severn Lodge*, he created a five-acre Japanese garden with fish ponds, rows of cherry trees and stone statuary. Entry was through a pillared gate built by Japanese gardeners, the only such construction in the West. He returned frequently to Japan. Bowie, Hillsborough's first Recorder (1910–1918), died in 1920. To the astonishment of local society, most of his estate was left to a Japanese wife and two sons whose existence had been unknown on the Peninsula until after his death.

Henry P. Bowie's Japanese garden

Quintessential clubman Francis Carolan married Harriet Pullman, daughter of railroad car magnate George Mortimer Pullman, in 1892. They moved to San Francisco, became members of the Burlingame Country Club and in 1897 built *Crossways*, a 30-room country seat at the junction of Willow Road and Sharon Avenue. The home had a tennis court, carriage house, terraced gardens and acres of lawn. Unlike husband Frank, Harriet Carolan was cold and aloof and not enamored with country club society. He built a private polo field. At one time he kept 94 trotters and polo ponies plus six of the finest carriage animals in the state. He relished fox hunting, bred English foxhounds and directed the colorful hunts. Harriet considered herself on a higher intellectual plane and had little to do with club activities. He was warm, gentle and, despite an arrest on neighbor complaints in 1917 because his kennel of 46 baying beagles disrupted local tranquility, one of the best liked men of his era.

Frank Carolan at Beaulieu

Poloist Frank Carolan

William H. Crocker, youngest son of the railroad builder and brother of Col. C.F. Crocker, was a dynamic force in the history of California and Hillsborough. On business in New York, April 1906, he was first to raise funds for the reconstruction of earthquake-ravaged San Francisco. He subsequently became known as "Mr. Banker" in the city and was a force in Republican politics. Few civic projects were undertaken without his approval. Crocker and his wife moved to a large home in Burlingame on Forest View Avenue in the early 1890s. Later they built elegant *New Place*, one of the town's more spectacular mansions. The Crockers had four children. Grandson Charles de Limur remembers Crocker as a "teddy bear," and that he perpetually ate the same breakfast: soft boiled egg, bacon, toast and marmalade—all mixed together in a bowl.

William H. Crocker at breakfast

Prince André Poniatowski and William H. Crocker

San Francisco banker William H. Crocker (right) and Prince André Poniatowski married sisters Ethel and Elizabeth Sperry, daughters of Stockton flour millionaire Austin Sperry. After 1895 the brothers-in-law involved themselves in business dealings financed by Crocker and promoted by Poniatowski. These enterprises ranged from racetrack ownership to the development of hydro-electricity. In 1897 they built the Blue Lake Powerhouse on the Mokelumne River to provide power to the Mother Lode. Their ultimate goal was to bring electricity to San Francisco. The Crocker - Poniatowski relationship disintegrated when the banker became critical of the prince's scheming and management style. Poniatowski forsook Burlingame in 1903, moving his family to France, where he became a banker. Crocker engineered a series of astute corporate mergers which, in 1905, became Pacific Gas & Electric.

Other than native oaks, the Burlingame hills were almost void of trees in the 1890's, as seen in this photograph of *Sky Farm*. The attractive wood home was commissioned by William H. Crocker in 1896 as a wedding gift for the Poniatowskis who, using the last three letters of their name, called it *Ski Farm*. But from the beginning, local residents insisted upon calling it *Sky Farm*. From 1910–1917 the William Bourn family rented the house. In the late '20s it was occupied by W.H. Crocker's son, William Willard Crocker and his family. It burned to the ground in 1928.

Ski Farm, **built in 1896**

Crossways Farm, Burlingame

Gymkhana events at the Burlingame Country Club

Until the eve of World War II, dressage and gymkhana caused genuine enthusiasm among Hillsborough residents. During early years regular competitions were held either on the country club lawn (pictured) or at Frank Carolan's *Crossways Farm* in west Burlingame. Later the events became increasingly formal and were moved to the *El Cerrito Polo Field*. Society writers and spectators flocked to see fashionable ladies displaying their newest, most delightful creations.

Local society found Prince André Poniatowski,
great great-grand nephew of the last king of
Poland and self-proclaimed heir to the Polish
throne, unusually fine looking and absolutely
regal with light brown hair, goatee, and long
mustache which he had the habit of twirling.
His passions were horse racing and highstakes
gambling. With W.H. Crocker's backing,
Poniatowski designed and built Tanforan
Park (San Bruno), a racetrack which opened in
1899. The prince had always been critical of
American raceways which he claimed lacked
the splendor of those in Europe. Thus Tanforan
was characterized by fine landscaping and
sweeping lawns. For decades Hillsborough's
horse-loving socialites flocked to San Bruno
to wager on the ponies. Much of the essential
business of the community was handled at the
track. The gloved, impeccable, business-like
Poniatowski is pictured while Walter Hobart
(in riding boots and spurs) conducts his affairs.
In the stable area is horse enthusiast Joseph
Oliver Tobin (center, in straw hat) having a
word with his brother Cyril.

Tobin party at the stables

**André Poniatowski and Walter Hobart
(wearing boots and spurs) at racecourse**

Riding in the Burlingame hills

Carolan swimming party at *Beaulieu*

In turn of the century Burlingame one had to love horseflesh or be socially damned. Debonair Frank Carolan was eminently comfortable in an equestrian society. Wife Harriet had to fake it. In 1909, longing for sophistication and bored with Burlingame, she purchased *Beaulieu*, the former Charles Baldwin estate in Cupertino. Small but classy, the place had orchards, sunken European gardens, sweeping lawns and a dramatic swimming pool. *Beaulieu* was a replica of *Le Petit Trianon* built in the park of Versailles, once the favorite residence of Marie Antoinette. Pictured is Carolan riding in the hills with Gertrude Murphy and an unidentified friend. Carolan is also shown entertaining friends at the Cupertino estate.

Clubman Walter Hobart helped introduce English-style fox hunting to Burlingame. Hunts, reeking of old world tradition, were splendid and colorful. For formal hunts, redcoated, black-velvet-capped huntsmen gathered at the Burlingame railroad depot and rode to the blast of the hunter's horn. The only item lacking locally was the fox. Burlingame terrain was ill suited, for the wily foxes usually managed to escape pursuers in heavy underbrush or deep ravines. For a time local coyotes were substituted, but with limited success. Finally it was discovered that a bag of anise could be dragged behind a horse to lay down a scent. This solved the fox problem and mitigated some of the rigors of the chase.

Gathering for a fox hunt

Coaching at *Crossways Farm*

Coaching parties before World War I were the fashionable set's most exhilarating amusement. Sportsmen Walter Hobart (at the reins) and Francis Carolan were probably most adept at handling the great four-in-hand coaches. Of all the activities in which Carolan participated, coaching was his favorite. He considered no expense too great. He owned 25 coaches, none cost less than $1,000. His collection included a *tally-ho* bought for a visit of William K. Vanderbilt and a big *Victoria* acquired especially to carry President Theodore Roosevelt from the Burlingame depot to lunch at the country club (1903). Coaching competitions at Carolan's *Crossways Farm* (located on what became the Burlingame High School field), elaborate all-day affairs, were high entertainment for local youngsters who gathered to watch richly liveried footmen perform with Prussian precision and ogle the gourmet feasts and fine wines served the visitors who came from the other side of County Road.

Much excitement along the Peninsula in 1902, when track layers completed construction of the San Francisco to San Mateo interurban streetcar. Service began Jan. 1, 1903, and before the day was done 900 people made the transit. Travel time from San Mateo to Market and Fifth streets was 60-75 minutes, depending on the time of day. Through fare was a quarter. Peninsula population soared. San Mateo Park, "a trolley car community" which opened in 1902, was advertised as "an easy walk to the streetcar." Many of Hillsborough's fashionable elite who worked in the city and were slaves to Southern Pacific's rigid timetables, preferred the streetcar's plebeian commute. Initially trolleys left hourly, later they ran 20 minutes apart from six in the morning to 1 a.m. Residents often were taken to the trolley in luxurious private carriages, as this picture of William H. Crocker attests. With the increase in automobile travel, ridership declined and service was discontinued Jan. 15, 1949.

Commuter William H. Crocker at the trolley stop

Every Republican president between Ulysses S. Grant and William Howard Taft found it financially and politically rewarding to make at least one pilgrimage to the San Francisco Peninsula during his term in office. On May 14, 1903, Theodore Roosevelt arrived amid appropriate military pomp and ceremony at the Burlingame depot, having accepted an invitation of country club members to lunch. He was driven to the club in the Carolan *Victoria*. The gray-uniformed boys of St. Matthew's Military School provided the honor guard. President Roosevelt's speech, greeted with wild cheering and enthusiastic applause, is reproduced in full: *"Let me thank you for coming out to see me, and say how I have enjoyed coming here. I have enjoyed being in California for the last week, and it has been the greatest possible pleasure."*

President Theodore Roosevelt at the Burlingame depot

Burlingame Club welcomes Theodore Roosevelt, 1903

Dapper Rudolph Spreckels (center), independent-thinking son of sugar magnate Claus Spreckels, was one of Hillsborough's most controversial personalities. Though businessman and millionaire in his own right, following the 1906 earthquake Rudolph donned a cloak of civic reformer, vowing to ferret out miscreants responsible for San Francisco's graft and corruption. When he attacked crooked politicians, better society supported him. However, upon declaring that *"corruption doesn't exist . . . unless supported by corrupt businessmen willing to pay for special privileges,"* influential men were outraged. Rudolph Spreckels' father and brothers turned against him. William H. Crocker, speaking for the social elite, called Spreckels a *"vicious reformer"* who employed *"passionate, revengeful and criminal methods."* His family was socially ostracized. At Pacific Union Club and at Burlingame Spreckels was declared *"diseased."* The family lived in Hillsborough until his wife's death in 1949. He moved to a three-room San Mateo apartment until his own death in 1958. Fellow clubman Frank Carolan is to the right of Spreckels.

Walter S. Hobart, Rudolph Spreckels and Frank Carolan

Edward M. Greenway

Eleanor Martin

By the early 20th century the Bachelor's Cotillion, a traditional kick-off of the winter season where the daughters of the social elect were presented to society, had become the year's most prestigious event. It had grown since 1887, when established by society matron Eleanor Martin and San Francisco's "social czar," Edward M. Greenway (pictured). No great fan of Eleanor Martin, editor Frances Moffat wrote that she sailed through society with the *"serene authority of a battleship."* Greenway and Martin issued the coveted cotillion invitations. A summons signaled acceptance by society. To be omitted meant one could *never belong*. Even before World War I, access to elite circles had become so rigid, eligibility was hereditary. For acceptance a young lady had to be descended from a member of a Greenway Cotillion. A new dynasty was created. Marriages between member families were both encouraged and frequent. From high society's standpoint, Greenway was the Peninsula's most powerful and feared man.

Irish-born Richard Tobin (1832) came to California with his parents during the Gold Rush. He read law in San Francisco and was admitted to the bar (1853). Along with several other San Franciscans, including his brother Robert J. Tobin, he organized the *Hibernia Savings & Loan Society* in 1859, serving as attorney for the society until his death at age 55 (1887). He was survived by a wife and seven children. The family became one of the most influential on the greater Peninsula. In 1906 it gathered at *El Palomar*, the San Mateo estate of Charles and Celia Clark (Richard's daughter), for the christening of their daughter Mary. Pictured standing are Agnes Tobin (a daughter of the founder), Father Charles Ramm, Archbishop Patrick W. Riordan, a nurse, Celia Tobin Clark (with daughter Mary), Charles Clark, Mrs. Richard Tobin (*the Mater*, wife of the founder), May Diamond (Mrs. Joseph Sadoc Tobin) and Beatrice Raoul-Duval (sister of Celia). Seated are Richard's sons Clement, Joseph Sadoc (holding Elizabeth Raoul-Duval), nephews Cyril (with Madeleine Raoul-Duval), Joseph Oliver Tobin, and sons Richard M. and Edward J. Tobin.

The Tobin family at *El Palomar*

Aficionados like to argue about the origin of American golfing. Some claim it was in Foxburg, Pennsylvania in 1885. Perhaps the country's first important course was St.Andrews, laid out in a Yonkers, New York apple orchard, 1888. Shortly after the establishment of the Burlingame Country Club, John Parrott II (son of the Gold Rush banker) and his brother-in-law Albert H. Payson conceived the idea for a three-hole course which was laid out in the treeless hills west of the club. The wind played havoc with the balls. Golfers played until they got dizzy. A nine-hole course was in use by 1900 and an 18-hole course 12 years later. James Melville, the country club's first golf professional, was hired in 1899 at a salary of $1.25 a day.

Cyril Tobin at the Charles W. Clark estate

Burlingame Club members were a fun loving albeit influential group which, according to early reports, paid dues reluctantly. Short of expulsion, directors tried every ploy, including the confiscation of horses and buggies stored in the club stables, to bring about compliance. Secretary Frank Carolan even wrote members' mothers attempting to collect. The fellows acquired reputations as playboys and marathon drinkers. John Parrott II shot an arrow into the nose of a buffalo head hanging over the club bar. Celebrating a victory at Coronado in March 1906, poloist Walter Hobart rode Cyril Tobin's horse (pictured) into the club. The prancer *"began the ascent of the highly polished stairs leading to the floor above, never missing a step . . . visited rooms of sleeping members . . . and made the precarious descent."* Club directors favored equestrian feats, but not on the second floor of the club. Hobart and Tobin were fined $25 each.

Hillsborough folks were dog people. Frank Carolan kept beagles and supervised breeding of English foxhounds. The Chesebroughs raised Airedales. Frances Murphy and daughter Gertrude were especially fond of standard poodles. The town's most renowned dog fancier was Jennie Crocker. She was known for her Boston bulls and whippets. After 1940 she was recognized as the premier Lakeland terrier aficionado in the nation. Her dogs always came first. They had the run of the house. Before marrying Malcolm Whitman (1912), concerned for her 65 canines, she asked him to sign a pre-nuptial understanding, agreeing to protect and respect her animals and to do nothing to estrange them from their beloved mistress. The couple honeymooned aboard her elegantly furnished private railroad car. When Whitman wanted to visit his wife, he did so in an adjoining car—brought along especially to accommodate all 65 dogs.

Youthful Jennie Crocker

Fire ravaged the luxurious Burlingame Club building on the morning of March 4, 1910. Members formed a bucket brigade and valiantly fought the flames. San Mateo and Burlingame fire units were unable to save it. Boys from nearby St. Matthew's Military School assisted finely dressed society matrons saving elegant furnishings and art objects. So grateful were club members for the assistance that upon meeting several of the 14-year old cadets in San Mateo, they rewarded them with beer from a local saloon. Neither St. Matthew's headmaster William Brewer nor the San Mateo police were amused by the show of gratitude. The country club fire spurred the creation of a Hillsborough Fire Department.

Burlingame Country Club fire, 1910

View of Hillsborough from C. Templeton Crocker's *Uplands*

Thirty-one communities in the United States officially are named *Hillsborough* or, more commonly, *Hillsboro*. Most, incorporated villages or towns, were so called because of their locations nestled in hills. Local legend has it that Hillsborough, California was named after *Hillsboro*, New Hampshire, said to be the home of early pioneer William Davis Merry Howard. Town founders apparently never made this connection, at least not officially. The quaint explanation, the source of which is unknown, appeared long after the town's incorporation. Howard was a native of Boston.

Perhaps Hillsborough's most revered building was her first town hall, allegedly built as a home by William Davis Merry Howard, a pioneer landowner in the early 1850s. The traditional story is that timbers used in construction were brought around Cape Horn. After Howard's death (1856), his widow, Agnes, married his brother George. They added on to the humble residence, located at De Sabla Road and Sherwood Court, and named the spacious new construction *El Cerrito*. In the early 20th century, in order to make way for the far grander Eugene de Sabla mansion, also called *El Cerrito*, the original was moved to Roehampton and Richmond roads, where for years it was the town hall, fire department and original public school. It was ultimately demolished in 1930.

Hillsborough's first town hall

Henry Tiffany Scott in 1926

Home of Henry T. Scott on Forest View

Dean of San Francisco finance and chairman of the board of directors of the Pacific Telephone and Telegraph Co., Henry Tiffany Scott was a founder of the country club and the town of Hillsborough; an original member of the board of trustees and the town's second mayor. The cigar-smoking Scott, who went to work for Union Iron Works during the 1860s, believed that San Francisco Bay was the finest place in the world to build ships. He later served as company president and earned the sobriquet *Builder of the Oregon* after successfully completing the modern battleship, which won international prominence during the Spanish-American War (1898) and the global cruise of the Great White Fleet (1908). Scott's program of warship construction advertised San Francisco's industrial potential, resulting in millions of dollars in contracts while acting as a wake up call to the complacent but supposedly invincible Philadelphia and Boston shipbuilders. Scott's beautiful home was on Forest View Avenue.

Fireman Walter Wisnom at the country club

Walter Wisnom, who went to work as a fireman for Hillsborough in 1920, poses on the bumper of the engine then housed in the country club stables on Floribunda Avenue. Wisnom often reminisced about practicing with the heavy engine, navigating the steep, one-way dirt road from Redington to Sky Farm. Fire was the town's most enduring problem, causing more than a million dollars of damage in its first years. The Joseph D. Grant, Charles W. Clark and Daniel T. Murphy homes were among the losses. When Murphy's burned in May 1910, the only stream of water played on the inferno came from a Burlingame Country Club hose, rushed there by Walter Hobart in his car. A fire committee consisting of C.T. Crocker, George Howard Jr. and Norris K. Davis had been formed in 1910 and owners of large estates were to maintain fire fighting equipment. An American La-France chemical engine was ordered in 1912 and the first fire chief, Walter A. Grant, was hired in May 1913. Police and fire departments were combined later that year.

**Lewis Hobart with the Bishop of Winchester at
Grace Cathedral, 1929**

Willis Polk

Architect Lewis P. Hobart, who married Mabel Deming (first cousin of Mary Deming Crocker—wife of the railroad tycoon), came west in 1906. He gained a reputation rebuilding structures in San Francisco's downtown. W.H. Crocker commissioned him to design *New Place* (completed 1909). His other notable Hillsborough homes included *Villa Rose* (later called *Strawberry Hill*) for Joseph D. Grant, *Rosecourt*, George Cameron's home and *Newmar* for George Newhall. After the 1906 fire destroyed their Nob Hill mansion, the Crockers donated the property to the Episcopal diocese and Hobart designed Gothic-styled Grace Cathedral, his only church.

"I am one of the most competent men in my profession, and when it comes to originality, Michelangelo has nothing on me," architect Willis Polk once declared. Rash, impulsive and outspokenly naive, with an extraordinary ability to insult, Polk was nonetheless talented. One of the Peninsula's *in* architects, he designed the Carolans' $200,000 clocktowered stables (1899) along with their polo pavilion, and supervised construction of the *Carolands* on Black Mountain, 1914. He was the primary designer of C. Templeton Crocker's *Uplands* and the reconstruction of St. Matthew's Episcopal Church following the 1906 destruction.

The George H. Howard Jr. estate at the end of Roehampton Road

George H. Howard Jr., though lacking specialized training, became one of the Peninsula's renowned architects and is credited with designing almost 75 buildings in Hillsborough and surrounding communities. A local personality, he was son of pioneers George and Agnes Howard, and a founding member of the country club. Looked upon as thinking and artistic, Howard often used half-timbered Tudor styling in his houses. Among his achievements were the George Shreve house at 245 El Cerrito Avenue (later sold to W.P. Fuller, Jr.), the house at 355 Hillsborough Blvd. (one-time home of adventure-writer Stewart Edward White) and the pavilion for the San Mateo Polo Club on El Cerrito. One of Howard's best known structures was the Burlingame railroad depot. Howard's own massive estate, located at the end of Roehampton Road, lacked the artistic appeal found in his other creations. Howard died in 1932. Five years later that estate was subdivided.

George H. Howard Jr.

In 1911 Hillsborough town trustee and treasurer C. Templeton Crocker married the striking Helene Irwin, daughter of Hawaiian sugar millionaire William G. Irwin. As a wedding present the delighted Irwin presented the couple with a check for $1 million. Soon after the marriage Crocker retained architect Willis Polk and began construction of a grand new mansion, *Uplands*, which he felt would place him on an equal social level with his uncle William H. Crocker and others who had built grandiose homes. To be close to their daughter, the Irwins moved to *Crossways*, until recently the home of Francis and Harriet Carolan. Though the Crocker union appeared solid and their new home became a place of grand entertainments, Helene soon charged that she was being ignored by the withdrawn and introspective Templeton, who lived much of his time elsewhere. The couple was divorced during the early 1920s. She subsequently married Paul Fagan.

Templeton (left) and Helene Crocker (center)

Beverly Sebanc and daughter Stacey in music room of *Rosecourt*

Rosecourt

Unlike most of the house and gardens at *Rosecourt*, which are decidedly French in character, the music room is Spanish, said to have been removed in 1925 from a 15th century village castle outside of Seville. Few chambers in Hillsborough have the same mystique. Arturo Toscanini played the panio and on a number of occasions Lily Pons sang. American baritone Lawrence Tibbett met his future wife there after a performance. Beverly Sebanc, wife of Allan Sebanc who purchased the house from the Cameron estate, plays a harp duet with daughter Stacey.

Once reached through iron gates and a winding, poplar-lined driveway, *Rosecourt*, designed by architect Lewis P. Hobart on a seven-acre expanse, was considered one of the most elegant houses in Hillsborough. It was the home of George and Helen Cameron. She was a daughter of *Chronicle* publisher Michael H. de Young. George Cameron later served as publisher. The house, French in character, was distinguished by its pink color and massive cobblestoned courtyard, reminiscent of 19th century Europe. At one time the cobblestones were part of San Francisco's California Street in front of Michael de Young's mansion. When that house was destroyed, Helen Cameron had the stones hauled to Burlingame to be included in her own courtyard.

Wedding Party

Mr. and Mrs. Malcolm Whitman

Wedding guests at reception pavilion

"Simplicity will be the keynote of my wedding" declared heiress Jennie Crocker, announcing plans to marry tennis great Malcolm Douglas Whitman at St. Matthew's Episcopal Church (San Mateo). The July 16, 1912, event became *the* social extravaganza of the decade, involving just 300 of the couple's "dearest friends." Noted architect George H. Howard Jr. designed a reception pavilion which was constructed on the front lawn of Jennie's rustic estate, *Home Place*. The $20,000 floral temple, with two rows of pillars supporting a balustrade, was hand painted with "liquid stone" resembling marble. *"No fairer setting could have been born in the brain of a poet,"* rhapsodized the *Examiner*. Guests breakfasted on sautéed frog legs, jellied pheasant and boned squab while toasting the couple with imported wines. Cameramen recorded every breathtaking minute. The pavilion was destroyed immediately after the reception. The couple was divorced in 1921.

W.P. Fuller family

In Northern California, noted for fogs and cool damp nights, paint peddlers stood to be millionaires. And William Parmer Fuller, who came west searching for gold, found it in a paint can. Though he started business in Sacramento in the early 1850s, operations were moved to San Francisco in 1862. Well before his death (1890), the pioneer paint dealer controlled one of the nation's most powerful concerns dealing in paint, oils and glass, dominating absolutely the business of the Pacific Coast. During the '70s, his company (in partnership with W. Frank Whittier) commenced local paint manufacture and in 1899 William P. Fuller II (never junior) opened a new 40-acre industrial complex in South San Francisco. The Fullers, many of whom called Hillsborough home, maintained control of the family business until 1962. One Fuller home in Hillsborough was on Brewer Drive (pictured, left, is Mrs. W.P. Fuller II). In 1925 the family purchased a large residence on El Cerrito Avenue. Shown also (in automobile) is W.P. Fuller Jr. (son of W.P. Fuller II), his aunt, Mrs. Frank Wastie Fuller, and family chauffeur George Loane.

Hillsborough children, 1912

Gertrude Murphy

Hillsborough youngsters in the decades before World War II saw little of their parents. Their needs were normally taken care of by nurse or governess. Most didn't dine with parents until they'd reached age 11 or 12. Traditionally, boys went away to boarding school after the 8th grade; girls were given somewhat longer at home. Juliette Bichon's responsibility as governess to *Miss Helen* and *Miss Ethel*, daughters of the William H. Crockers, was the girls' cultural education. French-born Juliette taught language, music and dance. There were annual visits to the continent—Paris for voice lessons and Bois de Boulogne for equestrian training. She accompanied the girls on vacations with French cousins and took them to call on family friends William and Agnes Bourn on the Lakes of Killarney in southern Ireland. Pictured are baby Gertrude Murphy and town children lined up for the camera in 1912.

Burlingame Country Club, circa 1919

The back veranda of the building which served as the Burlingame Country Club between 1912 and 1955 became its symbol. Furnished with green wicker tables, umbrellas and huge concrete urns of geraniums, it was *the* place for members to lunch. The club's guiding force, beginning in 1917, was Italian immigrant manager Mario Bona. He coordinated a staff of 50-60, supervised the kitchen and ran hotel services. Under his direction the club was reputed to be one of the most exclusive in the nation. Bona was absolutely devoted to club rules and never deviated. During Prohibition, when some members wanted to turn the place into a *speakeasy*, he forbade it and survived. To Bona, who always spoke with an Italian accent, it was a question of law, not morals. After repeal he won applause as a wine specialist. Members, grateful for all his efforts, built his family a Hillsborough home. Upon retirement in 1954, after 48 years on the job, Bona was allowed to purchase the house for $1,000.

Country club manager, Mario Bona

La Dolphine

George Almer Newhall

With entry to the grounds off Sharon Avenue, *Newmar* was guarded by heavy iron gates. The road to the house was bordered with four rows of towering Lombardy poplars. Designed along the lines of an Italian villa by Lewis Hobart (1913), the estate, characterized by formal gardens and spacious walks, was the home of millionaire importer-exporter George A. Newhall and wife Caroline. Newhall, outstanding in the civic affairs of San Francisco, had been president of the San Francisco Police Commission as well as the Presidio and Ferries Railways and the Chamber of Commerce. *Newmar*, renowned for showy gardens, covered 20 acres. The terrace to the south overlooked a long stretch of undulating lawn bordered by white and pink hawthorns. Below, a formal garden surrounded a large pool. Two tiers of clipped cypress hedges enclosed the entire expanse. Newhall died in 1929. A subsequent owner of the home, Dorothy Spreckels, entranced by a gold dolphin in one its many bathtubs, named the place *La Dolphine*, though there is no such word in French.

Carolands, circa 1920

Looking down on the Crockers . . . In 1910 Harriet Pullman Carolan dreamed about building a Napoleonic chateau to surpass William H. Crocker's *New Place* and other grand homes then planned by Templeton Crocker and George Newhall. She purchased 550 acres on Black Mountain and in 1914 began the *Carolands*, a one-million cubic-foot, 96-room chateau complete with a walk-in vault, two elevators and secret stairways for servants—the largest house on the Peninsula. Harriet and Francis Carolan occupied a small portion of the home in 1915, but lived there barely two years. Landscaping was never completed. Delicate French windows rattled in the wind which also whistled down chimneys, blowing soot in all directions. Elevators seldom worked. Flushing toilets sent the sound of rushing water echoing throughout the house. The furnace required three months to heat the place. The Carolans separated in 1917. She moved to the East. He died in 1923.

Frank and Harriet Carolan, Hillsborough's Lord & Lady Bountiful

Beagling at the *Carolands*, 1917

In 1916, at the prodding of ever energetic sports enthusiast Francis Carolan, athletic types introduced *beagling*, using packs of the small hounds to track jack rabbits across Hillsborough's rolling meadows with *beaglers* in hot pursuit on foot. For official competitions, beaglers wore spiffy green velvet coats with pale blue collars, white corduroy knickers, heavy green woolen hose and white spats. Caps were green with black ribbon bows dangling down their backs. Beagling never caught on, even in athletic Burlingame. While pursuing the hounds chasing the hares was wonderful fun, the crafty rabbits always got away and beaglers perpetually returned mud covered and with fancy clothing torn. Observers appreciated the shenanigans perhaps more than participants.

Beagle watching

More than any single event, the Panama-Pacific International Exposition of 1915 brought metropolitan sophistication to Hillsborough. Country club and great estates became social centers for visitors from the Atlantic states—the likes of Mrs. William K. Vanderbilt and young multi-millionaire Vincent Astor. *"We expected Eastern society to be enthusiastic about our exposition and its elaborate functions but weren't wholly prepared for their spontaneous appreciation of Peninsula pleasures,"* gushed a local swell. Many exposition polo matches were played on Peninsula fields. Horses involved in other equestrian events were stabled in Hillsborough, where facilities were *appropriately comfortable.* Special cars were attached to Southern Pacific trains to transport the thoroughbred horses to exposition events in San Francisco.

Exposition Society, 1915

St. Matthew's Military School cadets, circa 1914

Young pupils at St. Matthew's Military School, 1914

Uniforms and emphasis changed significantly at St. Matthew's Military School over the years. When the institution moved to Hillsborough in the 1890s, boys still wore traditional gray of Civil War styling. In 1914, during the school's twilight years but well before American involvement, new khaki uniforms reflected the local drive for preparedness and the growing community support for active American participation in World War I. A year before the school finally closed its doors in 1915, even the youngest cadets were receiving training in gas warfare, digging trenches and constructing wire entanglements.

Poniatowski children, prior to 1903

André Poniatowski and sons while serving France, 1914

Though André Jr., Stanislaus and Casimir Poniatowski, nephews of the William H. Crockers, were born and spent their early years in Burlingame, their parents forsook the Peninsula in 1903 for Europe, where Prince André served for a time as president of the French Bank of America. Before leaving, the three boys were photographed playing at Crocker's home on Forest View Avenue. When war broke out in 1914, the three, along with their father, enlisted in the French army. The boys fought on the Western Front. Prince André, commissioned a major, made frequent trips to America, generating financial support for the French cause. All survived the war. Following the armistice, Casimir returned to live near Santa Barbara.

Dance instruction, 1916

Patricia Tobin's dance class, 1916 . . . For Hillsborough youngsters, instruction in ballroom dancing has always been considered essential to a cultured upbringing. Classes came to be known as *white gloves* because little ladies were required to wear white gloves and young gentlemen neckties. One-time Police Chief William Key recalls Wednesday afternoon sessions during the 1950s with *"rotund, gregarious Frank Kitchen who taught with his glass of Scotch in hand."* He was *"very demanding, insisted on proper decorum . . . and tolerated neither nonsense nor wall flowers."* Cotillions were held at the Hillsborough Racquet Club. *"One hour classes seemed like six,"* says Key. Most boys hated them. Patricia Tobin is fourth from the right.

Gertrude Murphy

John Fuller and Betty Leight Wright

Raising Money . . . for Britain and France between 1914 and 1917 became a Peninsula passion which only increased after the United States declared war on Germany in April 1917. Just three weeks after the declaration socialites Walter Hobart, Francis Carolan, William Tevis and Christian de Guigné staged *the society event of the year*, a polo match at El Cerrito Field. Price of admission was 50 cents for the 1,000 who attended, proceeds going to support the American Red Cross. John Fuller and cousin Betty Leight Wright (pictured) passed the bucket for contributions. Gertrude Murphy, daughter of Eugene and Frances Hopkins Murphy, appeared as a French peasant in a patriotic melodrama put on by Hillsborough school children as their contribution to the war effort.

In a surge of patriotism accompanying the beginning of World War I, Hillsborough aristocrats vied with one another in public demonstrations of Americanism. W.H. Crocker fired all foreign born servants at *New Place* unless they agreed to become citizens. Harriet Carolan was the first to hire a woman chauffeur after hers was drafted into service. Much acreage at *Carolands* was transformed into a giant *victory garden*, mostly potatoes, grains and hay. Women drove for the Red Cross. On July 4, 1917, lumber tycoon George A. Pope staged a patriotic garden gala at his sprawling Geri Lane estate. Chartered trains transported honored guests, 2,000 officers and men from Camp Fremont in nearby Menlo Park. Hillsborough's patriotic elite turned out in sunbonnets and white shoes, adding color and gaiety to the afternoon event.

Near the front, 1918

Helen Chesebrough

Sisters Edith and Helen Chesebrough moved into their new Hillsborough home on Brewer Drive in 1916. Both were active in the American Red Cross. Edith subsequently married former Naval intelligence officer and stockbroker William C. Van Antwerp (Dec. 20, 1920) and moved to a new palatial home on Easton Drive the next year. Helen joined the Red Cross Canteen Service during World War I and, in 1918, was sent to France to serve soldiers on the Western Front. She returned to become Vice Chairman of the San Mateo County Chapter of the Red Cross and Chairman of Volunteers, positions she maintained until her death in 1949. Helen Chesebrough never married and was commonly known as *Miss Red Cross of San Mateo County*. She is pictured formally in the uniform of the Canteen Service and (left front) with American soldiers on a station platform in France.

Edmund Parrott **Josephine Parrott** **John Parrott** **Joseph Parrott** **William G. Parrott**

The Parrotts of Baywood . . . Few families were as actively involved in World War I. *Archibald Dick* and *Ralph Gladwin*, Scots Guards, son and son-in-law of Archibald Douglas Dick and wife, the former Edith Isabel Parrott (daughter of Gold Rush banker John Parrott), fell in battle, 1915. *Edmund Parrott*, the banker's grandson (scion of John Parrott II), a U.S. aviator, was killed when his plane was shot down behind German lines. His younger brother *Joseph Parrott*, an ambulance driver on the Western Front before American entry into the war, returned to join the Army. He died of influenza at Camp Fremont in Menlo Park weeks before the war's end. Their sister *Josephine Parrott*, one of the first women authorized to serve in the U.S. Navy, was a Yeomanette stationed in Washington, D.C. Brother *William G. Parrott* was also a flier and *John Parrott* served in the artillery. Another brother, *Francis Parrott*, died in an automobile accident on El Camino Real in 1918.

Mrs. Leslie Whitney and Mrs. Harold Mack

There was a definite role for the turn of the century Hillsborough woman. Be prominent at polo matches, musicales, socials and religiously attend meetings of the Garden Club. Assiduously avoid political and social discussions and remain always in the shadow of one's husband. *Cecelia Cudahy Casserly* refused to conform. In summer 1918, when hospitals were overwhelmed with victims of Spanish influenza, she headed the Red Cross relief committee, shocking neighbors by opening her own home on Bridge Road to sufferers. During the worst three weeks of the epidemic, 57 people were treated and nine died there. The following year she continued to raise eyebrows in the millionaire community, publicly supporting striking telephone operators. In 1928 she became the first local woman to run for Congress, her platform being *"equal pay for women performing the same duties as men,"* and *"to help women gain the rights to which they are entitled."* She lost. Pictured at the Burlingame depot is a unit of the San Mateo County Red Cross Motor Corps. At right is commandant Mrs. Harold Mack with adjutant Mrs. Leslie Whitney (of the Leslie Salt fortune).

Cecelia C. Casserly

When it came to financial titans, few surpassed
Hillsborough resident Joseph D. Grant. He
pioneered the development of hydroelectricity,
the California oil industry and steel production
in the West. After his Burlingame home burned
(1909), he commissioned Lewis Hobart to
design *Villa Rose* (subsequently called *Strawberry
Hill*), built on a Hillsborough hilltop surrounded
by 50 forested acres. An avid sportsman, Grant
was devoted to polo and golf—both games he
helped introduce to the Peninsula. But it was in
his determination to protect California's *Sequoia
sempervirens* (Coast Redwoods), which he
found *"incomparably nobler, more beautiful and
more serene than any [temple] erected by the hands
of man,"* that Grant left an indelible imprint.
*"The heritage we pass to our children must not be
less than what we have received,"* he declared in
1917. *"The big trees are making their last stand."*
Two years later he helped form the Save-the-
Redwoods League, dedicated to preserving the
majestic giants. Until his death (1942) he was
a major contributor to the cause. The *Joseph
D. Grant Grove,* in the Del Norte coast region,
one of the most magnificent stands of *Sequoia
sempervirens* in the state, is his living memorial.

J.D. Grant Grove, Del Norte Coast Redwoods State Park

Joseph D. Grant

Tea dancing at the *Uplands*

F. Scott Fitzgerald was the author of choice during the early '20s and *jazz dancing* was in. Victorian morals and restrictions were things of the past. The *new woman* liberated herself from the corset and indulged in makeup, loose fitting dresses, intimate dancing and drinking. Women were drawn to smoking, the *cause célèbre* which many thought would make them equal to men. Hillsborough couples are shown on the veranda of C. Templeton Crocker's *Uplands* demonstrating their well-poised liberality.

Well-poised liberality

Burlingame Country Club

For years the country club was virtually Hillsborough's community center. Old-timers fondly remember 4th of July celebrations when members and guests from surrounding towns gathered on the veranda to watch fireworks detonated above the golf course. Much excitement Jan. 17, 1911, when aviators James Radley, flying a Bleriot monoplane, and Walter Brookin, at the controls of a Wright biplane, flew from Tanforan to the country club. Invited for *tea,* they said. Smart setters were fascinated with aviation. In December 1912, popular society matron Mrs. Eugene Murphy made friends green with envy by becoming the first local woman to go aloft, flying with birdman Roy Francis on a personalized tour of Peninsula polo fields and country clubs. During the '20s it wasn't uncommon for aviator-members, notably the W.P. Fuller family, to land on the club's golf course and taxi in to partake of lunch and refreshment.

Frances Hopkins Murphy and daughter Gertrude

Bellevue Avenue and the County Road, 1924

"A marvelous modern device . . ." is the way everybody referred to the *Martel Automatic Traffic Signal* installed at the busy corner of Bellevue Avenue and the County Road April 15, 1924, amid much official pomp and ceremony. The signal, voted on by the Hillsborough town council following a series of particularly nasty automobile accidents, had a revolving arm bearing the word *STOP* for daytime use and red and green semaphore lights for after dark. An added safety feature was a resonant bell which sounded both day and night. The signal was operated manually by a police officer who stood in a sentry box on the corner or it could work automatically. Mr. A.F. Martel of Burlingame told Hillsborough trustees that he installed the light *"at a large expense knowing that nothing is too good for your class of people. . ."*

Pacific Telephone & Telegraph

Pacific Telephone and Telegraph built the building at 1600 Floribunda Ave. in 1917 to serve as the telephone exchange providing service to homes in Hillsborough, Burlingame and San Mateo. Because of town charter restrictions on business, the building was given a Burlingame address. In 1926 Pacific Telephone moved to a larger new building on Burlingame Avenue. At that time the structure was modified and expanded to serve as Hillsborough's town hall. Its address was changed and again made officially part of Hillsborough.

Hillsborough Town Hall

By the mid 1920s, Hillsborough town offices had outgrown their first home in the old house at Richmond and Roehampton roads which had served as a combination fire and police department and public school. On July 6, 1926, Scott Martin raised the American flag during opening day ceremonies at the new Hillsborough Town Hall at 1600 Floribunda Avenue.

Along the length of San Francisco's Peninsula, where his power was omnipresent, Michael H. de Young's clan was commonly referred to as the *royal family.* De Young and his brother Charles established the San Francisco *Chronicle* during the 1860s, a newspaper devoted to sensationalism and exposé, often at the expense of truth and ethics. Nevertheless, de Young's daughters married into some of the Peninsula's most elite families. Kathleen (1888–1954), with her head on the publisher's shoulder, became Mrs. Ferdinand Thieriot; Constance (1885–1968) married Joseph Oliver Tobin; baby Phyllis (1891–1988) went to the altar with Nion Tucker; Helen (1883–1969) wedded George Cameron. *Legend* has it that even though de Young had gradually shed his sinister reputation to become one of the city's leading citizens, his sons-in-law at the Burlingame Club were required to pledge they would never bring him into the institution's sacrosanct halls — even as a guest. De Young's daughters, at first cautiously regarded in Hillsborough, became some of the Peninsula's most philanthropic and respected women. Also pictured is the girls' brother Charles (1881–1913) and Mrs. Michael de Young (1857–1917). The sisters-Phyllis Tucker, Constance Tobin and Helen Cameron-are shown on an outing at the De Young Museum in 1961.

Mrs. Tucker, Mrs. Tobin and Mrs. Cameron

El Cerrito Polo Field, 1913

Washington's Birthday, 1908 . . . great excitement. The new polo field of the San Mateo Polo Club at El Cerrito Park is opened. Richard Tobin, who has played on nearly all the best fields in the world, declares it the *"best in the state;"* that he has never played *"on a finer, springier field anywhere."*

Financier-industrialist Joseph D. Grant was one of the first to introduce polo to the Peninsula. During the early years *"our polo ponies were converted broncos . . . who played the game better than we did . . . they could turn on a dime,"* he wrote. English poloists had fancy pigskin saddles; in Burlingame players used ill-adapted Mexican saddles. The sport, which ranked high in the outdoor life of early California, became increasingly sophisticated until, in the years after World War I, the Peninsula was recognized as the world center of the equine sport. Teams from England, Australia and Argentina as well as the East Coast came to play championship matches. In addition to Tobin and Grant, local clubmen Walter Hobart, Frank Carolan and William Tevis were among the top performers. Above, virtually all of Hillsborough's high society gathered on the veranda of the San Mateo Polo Club in 1913 to watch the action and have their photograph taken.

Polo, *the Sport of Kings*, was the rage of early Burlingame and Hillsborough. Because of the area's undulating hills and numerous trees, adequate land for fields was scarce. Most competitions were held on privately owned property in Burlingame or San Mateo. Weekend matches were high society events. Young socialites considered acquiring a polo vocabulary part of their social equipment. While sleek poloists on elegant mounts thundered up and down the fields, chic, expensively dressed women sipped beverages from crystal goblets on the sidelines. Village children circled as close as they dared to watch. Popping of corks led them to the conclusion that the drink of choice was champagne.

Consuelo (Nini) Tobin

El Cerrito Field was also the scene of dressage and gymkhana events during the 1920s. Pictured is Consuelo (Nini) Tobin, daughter of Joseph Oliver Tobin and granddaughter of Michael H. de Young, sitting atop *Gypsy* at El Cerrito, circa 1920. She later became Mrs. Francis A. Martin Jr.

Before World War II most Hillsborough families relied on live-in help. In full operation, William H. Crocker's *New Place*, with 12 bedrooms and 10 baths, averaged 65 servants—20 inside and 45 in the garden. The domestic's world was as structured as the millionaire society itself. The *housekeeper* coordinated everything, supervised staff and was in charge of sewing and linens, while being the only servant addressed by last name. She prepared the house budget and, if efficient, the master was never disturbed with details. The *butler* waited table, was in charge of silver and answered the door. There were *upstairs maids*, *downstairs maids*, *kitchen maids* and at least one *chauffeur*. All the servants helped raise youngsters. However, just below the *housekeeper* was the *governess*, with primary responsibility for children. She was addressed by first name at home and as *Miss* while traveling. Pictured are five Crocker servants on an outing in one of the master's autos. Shown also is Juliette Bichon, *governess* to Crocker's daughters and later country club *housekeeper*.

Crocker domestics

Juliette Bichon

Of all Peninsula ethnic minorities, none was more discriminated against than the Chinese. Until after World War II Chinese were seen only as laborers and domestics. Commonly, the old families desired Chinese cooks and laundrymen. During the 1880s, Scotsman John McLaren used Chinese work gangs to create showy estate gardens. Hard labor—hauling dirt or gravel, building roads and stone walls as well as tree planting, wood cutting, and plowing—was accomplished by the Asians. Reservoirs and irrigation systems facilitating cultivation of the town's outstanding gardens were exclusively built by Chinese. The town's ethnic composition changed after the '60s. In 1963 Jack Ken, a University of California graduate, son of a San Bruno flower grower, became the first Chinese to buy property and build a home. In subsequent years the town became a goal for well-to-do Chinese professionals the likes of Dr. Lin Ho and wife Jennifer (pictured), who viewed Hillsborough as ideal for raising children. During the 1980s, this population expanded by growing numbers of immigrants from Hong Kong, Singapore and Taiwan. Shown also is Li-Hing-Chang (c. 1920), personal cook to William H. Crocker at *New Place*. Proud of the town's new cultural diversity, the four public schools unite annually for a community celebration of Chinese New Year.

Chinese New Year celebration at Crocker Middle School, 1991

Li-Hing-Chang, circa 1920

Lin Ho and wife Jennifer with Elizabeth and Juliana, 1991

Daniel Koshland

Koshland children among the hydrangeas

Not many children came to play with the Koshland kids during the 1920s; they were just too far out into the country, the only house atop Reservoir Road. Phyllis remembers the daily 20-minute walks with a girlfriend to Hillsborough school—down Reservoir to Bowhill Road, both unpaved, and east along El Cerrito Avenue. The best time of the year was late summer, when they would pause along the creek to gather wild blackberries. For Dan, Phyllis, and Sissy Koshland, pictured left to right amid the hydrangeas, their playground was the open grassy fields. Dan is shown also, circa 1927, with faithful companion *Spotty*, a special friend of unknown origin.

Hillsborough was known for the efficiency of its police department. During early years strangers driving through were often stopped and asked to explain their presence. Citizens regularly reported unexplained parked cars. Claude M. Hirschey, hired by the town in 1911, became police chief in 1926. For years he served in that role and as fire chief, health officer, building inspector and census taker as well. He remained chief until 1940 when, after disagreements with the town council, he simply faded into history. Early Hillsborough police patrols were often made in Cadillac roadsters. State crime reports of 1947 attest to the department's effectiveness in the millionaire community. Three burglaries were reported that year.

Hillsborough police on patrol

Royal visit at *New Place*, **1926**

As president of the Crocker National Bank, few local men of the 20th century exercised the same financial power and political influence as William Henry Crocker. A Yale graduate, he was a patron of the arts, president of the California Academy of Sciences and a backer of Steinhart Aquarium. He arranged the gift of Crocker family property to the Episcopal Church for the construction of Grace Cathedral. In 1910 his family occupied *New Place*, set amid 500 park-like acres. Designed by architect Lewis P. Hobart, it was said to be the *"most beautiful residence in California."* Crocker's guest books are filled with names of politicians, generals and other powerful potentates who visited the palatial estate up to the time of his death in 1936. Pictured are the Crown Prince and Princess of Sweden, with Ethel and William H. Crocker, upon departing *New Place* after a stay from July 27 – Aug. 4, 1926.

William Parmer Fuller
Jr. and friends . . . .

Country School, **1935. Bobby Hooker, My My Howard, unidentified, Diana Crocker, Laurie Wurmbrandt, Bob Henderson, Dale Cowgill, Lin Miller**

John and Parmer Fuller

Some parents weren't satisfied with Hillsborough's one public school and in 1929 created the private *Country School* for children of the elite. Oblivious to the onset of the depression, they purchased land near Crystal Springs Road and Alameda de las Pulgas. Progressive teachers for grades one through eight were hired in Winnetka, Illinois, to prepare charges for transfer to strict boarding schools. Emphasis was on acting, music and a general classical academic education. Children— many took afternoon golf lessons at the country club — were isolated from harsh realities of the depression. Students remember the butler and cook who fixed delicious lettuce sandwiches for snacks and served hot luncheon daily, as well as the morning and afternoon line-up of chauffeur-driven limousines. During the national hysteria following abduction of the Charles Lindbergh baby (1932), personal bodyguards accompanied many youngsters to class. The school closed in the late '30s.

Barbara Kahn at the *Gymkhana*

Nov. 30, 1929: residents hailed *"the next generation of polo players and expert horsewomen,"* as a score of Hillsborough youngsters displayed skill in horsemanship at the auspicious dedication of their new club, the *Gymkhana,* on 20th Avenue near the polo grounds in San Mateo. A flag raising ceremony, comments by Joseph Oliver Tobin, and a parade of young riders around the mile and a half track were features of the exercises. Many spectators attached special sentiment to the elaborate pavilion, now in a new location. It had once been part of the Charles W. Clark private race-course—in days of yore a setting of the Peninsula's most notable equestrian events. Formed by parents, the club encouraged horsemanship among juniors of the elite colony. Pictured is Barbara Kahn (Gardner), whose father was one of the backers. The organization lasted until the 1940s, when facilities burned in a spectacular blaze.

Bobby Henderson's (center with necktie) sixth birthday party, 1933

Scott Martin's birthday party, circa 1925

Birthdays were special occasions, often celebrated with extra-ordinary planning and care. Clowns or magicians were hired. Cooks prepared outdoor feasts. Festivities were under the watchful supervision of governesses. Lavish parties went beyond childhood. Mrs. Irvin Gardner, the former Barbara Kahn, daughter of Samuel Kahn, president of San Francisco's Market Street Railway, vividly recalls her 21st birthday party in 1939. Her father placed a trolley at her disposal—the gleaming white *President's Car,* trimmed in gold with wicker furniture upholstered in red velveteen. Frolicking guests were picked up at the end of the interurban line in San Mateo and sped up the Peninsula for an afternoon of tea dancing and levity at the Cliff House.

Swimming at Crocker Lake

Miller family at *Home Place*

Sons of Robert W. Miller

Opportunities for swimming in early Hillsborough were at best limited. For years, *Crocker Lake,* built as a reservoir by William H. Crocker to irrigate *New Place,* was the summertime mecca of Peninsula youngsters. Theoretically private and closed to all but the family and invited guests, guards were uncharacteristically inept in preventing trespassing. Kids gathered there from all over the surrounding area. Burlingame's Horace Jerome O'Keefe (pictured) enjoys a cool dip in 1923. The lake became especially renowned among servants of surrounding estates as a place for courtship.

In later years Robert and Jennie Crocker Henderson put in a pool at *Home Place.* Many members of the Hillsborough aristocracy remember it with special tenderness as the place where they learned to swim. Pictured in the foreground are Robert Watt Miller (in hat) and sons Robert Folger and Paul Miller. The Hendersons made something of a community center of *Home Place.* Site of the Hillsborough Garden Club's annual meeting, the pool area was regularly turned over to police and firemen for picnics. During World War II, Army and Navy officers made the 133-acre estate a virtual extension their officers' clubs.

Scarlet-coated Walter S. Hobart following the hounds across an open meadow, the trumpets of his grooms ringing out over the countryside. A common sight in the century's first decades. Handsome, dashing and fiery tempered, Hobart was the prototype of a millionaire clubman whose life was dedicated to polo, horse racing, yachting and big game hunting. He dabbled occasionally in real estate and mining. In later life Hobart, whose fortune was traced to his father's mining endeavors near Virginia City, Nevada, opened a dairy and became a gentleman farmer. By 1929 he was serving most wealthy homes of Hillsborough and delivering 2,250 gallons of milk and cream monthly to the St. Francis Hotel in San Francisco. Twice married, Hobart had two daughters (Hannah and Ruth) and a son (Walter) by his first marriage. A reluctant Ruth, at the prodding of her father, became the first wife of William Willard Crocker.

Hannah, Walter Hobart and Ruth

Hillsborough School Band, 1937

Hillsborough's first public school, established 1914, was in a single room of the one-time George Howard home. Moved from its original location to Roehampton and Richmond roads, the school shared quarters with town offices. In 1917 a new Hillsborough School opened on El Cerrito Avenue. Kindergarten through 8th grade classes were held in the easily recognized, stuccoed building, remembered for its heavy, Spanish-styled tile roof. The town's pride, it was destroyed in 1969 to make way for modern *South School*. Population growth after World War II demanded expanded educational facilities. *North Hillsborough School,* on part of William H. Crocker's *New Place* (one room sits atop the filled-in swimming pool) opened in fall, 1950. With subdivision of the former *Carolands* property, still more classrooms were required and *West Hillsborough School* on Black Mountain opened in 1954. Five years later, on property made available by the Crocker family, 7th and 8th grades were moved to the new *William H. Crocker Middle School* (6th grade was added to *Crocker School* in 1972).

At the *Woodland Theater*

As a sponsor of the Philharmonic Society of San Mateo County during the 1920s, socialite Cecelia Casserly approached Mrs. Lenora Armsby with the idea that Hillsborough should become a Bay Area cultural center. Casserly promoted the idea of building an amphitheater where the San Francisco Symphony would play summertime concerts. A wooded ravine adjacent to Hillsborough School on the bank of San Mateo Creek was chosen as the site. School trustees cooperated and construction began on *Woodland Theater,* a simple stage (on property owned by C. Templeton Crocker) surrounded by a grove of trees forming a sounding board for orchestra or chorus. Sailcloth netting covered a tiered theater, protecting as many as 2,000 listeners from afternoon sun. The first concert was held in June 1926, and throughout the '30s music lovers converged to appreciate music in an ideal outdoor setting. Over the years Woodland Theater was also used for school pageants and graduations.

Charles Templeton Crocker, grandson of railroader Charles Crocker and son of Col. Charles Frederick Crocker, was Hillsborough's first treasurer and on the original board of trustees. He married sugar heiress Helene Irwin (1911) and soon began building a massive, 37-room, $1.6 million country seat he called *Uplands*. In 1927, charging neglect, Helene sued for divorce. He retained *Uplands*, but preferred a two-floor, glass-enclosed penthouse apartment at 945 Green St. in San Francisco. Jean Michael Frank was commissioned to decorate the apartment in the French Art Deco style. Guests marveled at Crocker's panoramic view, aquariums of exotic tropical fish set level with the floor, semi-circular black tub and bathroom fixtures to match. Sheepskins served as wall hangings and furniture was upholstered in shark and camel skins. The dining table was made with crushed egg shells, baked and laboriously lacquered. Well before it was vogue, Crocker was considered one of America's leading Art Deco collectors. He never remarried.

Templeton Crocker and guests at *Uplands*

Templeton Crocker on the family's private car *Mishawaka*

House aficionados contend this distinguished mansion located along Tournament Drive is one of the last genuine Tudors to be built in America. Planned by Mrs. Celia Tobin Clark, daughter of Hibernia Bank founder Richard Tobin and former wife of Montana copper millionaire Charles W. Clark, *House-on-Hill* was designed in 1929 by architect David Adler, with construction completed two years later. The three-story, 47-room home was built during the Great Depression at extraordinary cost. Construction was done by hand; no power tools were permitted. Laborers even excavated the enormous basement with picks and shovels. Perhaps $1 million was funneled into the San Mateo economy. One planing mill, which ceased operation at the depression's outset, reopened after receiving an order for $150,000 in oak planking.

Formal gates frame the entranceway to *House-on-Hill*

William Orvik, Sgt. Walter Wisnom and Peter Lencioni

Hillsborough police and firemen still operated as one department when Walter J. Wisnom was hired in 1919. A *deputy marshall*, his first job was driving the fire engine, although he frequently patrolled streets on a motorcycle as well. After the departments separated (1938), Wisnom stayed with the police as a sergeant. When long-time chief Claude M. Hirschey left in 1940, legend has it that Wisnom walked into the chief's office, found a gold badge on the desk, pinned it on and didn't take it off for 20 years. He became police chief officially, Jan. 1, 1941. Wisnom was ideal for Hillsborough. Residents seldom were ticketed. Party goers who over-imbibed were driven home by police. Officers checked houses of vacationers, put licenses on bicycles and even visited homes to register people to vote. Wisnom seldom released information to the press. *"Crime, like marriage, is a private affair."* He retired in 1952. Pictured (during the '20s) is the combined department. A decade later are officers William Orvik, Sgt. Walter Wisnom and Peter Lencioni.

New Place

William H. Crocker's *New Place* was the first of the lavish Burlingame homes designed by architect Lewis P. Hobart. It was completed in 1909. There were 12 bedrooms and 10 baths upstairs. The estate was virtually self-sufficient. All the milk, butter, eggs, vegetables and fruit consumed at the house were grown or produced there. During the '20s and '30s, for actors and actresses, foreign diplomats and military leaders, politicians and presidents, a stay at *New Place* was *de rigueur*. Newspaper society scribes commonly referred to it admiringly as *New Place society*. W.H. Crocker's grandson, Charles Crocker de Limur, who spent much of his youth there, remembers *New Place* as "an extremely efficiently run hotel." During the 1950s the family *gave* the house to the Burlingame Country Club while *selling* the organization the land. The Crockers feared that any other arrangement would result in the destruction of the house.

William H. Crocker

William H. Crocker stayed in shape. He adored the Bohemian Club and loved golf, although he isn't remembered as having been a strong hitter. During the '20s and '30s he commuted daily to San Francisco by train. Burlingame residents remember that he rode horseback from *New Place*, deep in Hillsborough, to the Burlingame depot, never failing to bring a bag of nickels which he delighted in dispensing to Burlingame children who always flocked around him. A chauffeur followed with a groom who returned the mount to the stables. Now and then the horse was slowly trotted up Burlingame Avenue, tied to the back of the car. In his later years, after the death of his wife, the master of *New Place* went to the movies *every* night in San Mateo, Burlingame or Broadway, often seeing the same film four times. His seat was first row center of the balcony. A community favorite, the millionaire banker was never asked to pay for entry. Crocker died Sept. 25, 1937.

A gathering of notables, July 27, 1935 . . . Saturday afternoon at the Christenson home in Hillsborough. Across the terrace from the house and down a pathway marked by little round boxwood trees the bridal party walked between admiring friends to the outdoor altar set against spreading oaks.

In a town known for spectacular weddings, none was grander than the marriage of Christian de Guigné III, descended from a French noble family (his grandfather married Mary Katharine Parrott in 1897), to Eleanor Christenson, daughter of the lumber millionaire. The wide lawns were thronged with 700 smartly gowned guests. The wedding party, photographed after the Roman Catholic ceremony, included (left to right): Barbara Tobin (Thieriot), Edwin Christenson, Patricia Tobin (Cooper), Jane Christenson (de Tristan), Joseph Nelson, the bridegroom, Richard Tobin, the bride, Thomas A. Driscoll, Barbara Cates, Joseph de Dampierre, Evelyn Salisbury (Janir), Nichol Smith, Dale King (Christenson de Bonchamps), Marc de Tristan and Charles Christenson.

The Christian de Guigné and Eleanor Christenson wedding, 1935

Andrew Welch's formal garden

John McLaren

Andrew Welch, president of California & Hawaiian Sugar, created three separate gardens on his eight acre estate near Crystal Springs Road. One was authentically Japanese. Another was what he called a "Western garden," characterized by towering Coast Redwoods, banks of azaleas and lush ferns surrounding a pond and waterfall. The third was a more formal, rose-edged English sunken garden laid out by landscape architect *John McLaren* in 1908. Visitors, merely walking through gates, seemed to pass into different worlds.

Of all the landscape gardeners, *McLaren* was the most esteemed. A graduate of the Royal Botanical Gardens at Edinburgh, Scotland, he came to the Peninsula in 1872 to landscape George and Agnes Howard's *El Cerrito.* Until his death (1943), McLaren helped design many local estates, laid out some of the town's roads, planned San Mateo Park and landscaped nearby St. John's Cemetery, where many town pioneers are buried. McLaren became superintendent of San Francisco's Golden Gate Park (1887).

Pictured in the sunken garden, shortly after its completion, are Welch's wife Julia and daughters Florence and Marie.

Masasaburo Asai, a self-taught gardener born in Nagoya, Japan, who came to America in 1904, was hired in the 1930s by Andrew Welch to continue work on his Japanese garden, which had been started in 1914. Asai was chauffeured daily from his home in Oakland. Upon completing the Japanese segment, he helped design the "Western garden." Although the gardens were the inspiration of Welch's wife, the sugar executive derived tremendous pleasure from them. Asai often saw Welch, fully dressed in suit, stiff collar and tie, kneeling in the mud, floating model boats in the carp-filled ponds. Florence Bruce, Welch's daughter, remembers Asai as an artist and philosopher. *"He'd spend an entire day placing a single rock only to return the next, become dissatisfied and start all over again."* In Welch's gardens, authenticity was essential. He brought carpenters from Japan to build tea houses and bridges. Stone lanterns, bonsai trees and statuary were imported. Pictured is Welch's wife Julia, seated on the steps of the tea house in the Japanese garden. An artist in her own right, during the '30s Julia Welch found a moss covered, redwood, split rail hog fence near Napa. She acquired it by promising to build the hog farmer the most modern fence of whatever design he chose. The ancient fence was dismantled and rebuilt in the Western garden.

Tea house in the Andrew Welch Japanese Garden

Masasaburo Asai

Members of the Hillsborough Racquet Club

Athletic skill, whether on horseback or otherwise, has always been considered important in Hillsborough. Whereas many turn-of-the century residents favored the gentility of croquet, by 1937 some of the landed gentry opted for badminton when a handful of serious players rented the old San Mateo Polo Club on El Cerrito (for $75 a month) and were soon calling themselves the *Hillsborough Racquet Club*. Racqueteers, who managed to fit vigorous practice sessions in on Thursday nights between the social hour and dinner, regularly competed in state badminton championships, and at least one women's team traveled to Seattle for a tournament. Now recognized as one of the oldest organizations in the community, membership has traditionally been restricted, with new members admitted by invitation only.

The gentility of croquet

Hoffmann House

Arthur Hoffmann, 1937

Of all Hillsborough's venerable homes, only two are included on the *National Register of Historic Places* (although the *Town of Hillsborough Historic Building Survey* lists 13 others fitting the necessary criteria which haven't been submitted for recognition). The first listed was the *Carolands* (1975). The second was *Hoffmann House* on La Cuesta Road. It was added to the *National Register* in 1991. Designed by architect Richard Neutra and built in 1937, it is an example of *Neutra's High International Style*. Unique among Hillsborough homes, which tend toward classical, English and European designs, *Hoffmann House* features stark white, angular surfaces, set off by aluminum detail and dozens of windows. It was built originally for socialites Arthur (pictured) and Mona Hoffmann, well known in progressive and artistic circles of the 1930s.

Count and Countess Marc de Tristan with son Marc Jr., 1940

Hillsborough's crime of the century . . . Sept. 20, 1940. A daring mid-day kidnapping on a well-traveled street at the intersection of Poett Drive and Roehampton Road. Three year old Marc Louis Edwin de Tristan Jr., grabbed from the arms of his nurse by a pistol-packing abductor who slammed the nurse to the ground and sped off with the child in a 1936 Ford sedan. The missing boy, son of Count and Countess Marc de Tristan, was related to the Parrotts and Tobins (his godparents were Mrs. Charles Thieriot and Christian de Guigné III). The police investigation became the largest manhunt in Northern California history. The kidnapper managed to elude roadblocks, but the following day was sighted by an alert citizen and subsequently arrested. Little Marc was unharmed. Sixty hours after his disappearance the golden-haired, blue-eyed victim was reunited with his happy parents at their El Portal Road home.

The Burlingame Country Club

World War II. . . "For Hillsborough it was more than a war, it was a revolution," says Robert Folger Miller. *"Before Pearl Harbor we had at least a dozen servants in the house at any one time . . . then my father joined the Army and we moved. After the war, we returned; the servants never did. War doomed the Hillsborough lifestyle."*

The town fully supported the war effort. Resident Theodore Max Lilienthal headed up a county-wide campaign to collect tons of scrap, part of the government's *Salvage for Victory* drive. Fashionable women donned Red Cross uniforms. The old John Barneson mansion on Summerholme Place served as quarters for naval officers. Young ladies, who formed a chapter of American Women's Voluntary Services under Phyllis Tucker's leadership, operated the Naval Mess at the Howard Spreckels mansion on Floribunda Avenue, providing officers evening meals, dancing and entertainment. The country club acquired the air of an officers' club.

Ladies of the American Women's Voluntary Services at the Barneson mansion

Phyllis Tucker

Elizabeth Mack in Red Cross uniform

Officers' Mess at the John Barneson home

Caretaker Joe Travres, real estate agent H.A. Lang Jr. and new owner Tomlinson I. Moseley at *Carolands*, 1948

Even before the war, the sun was setting on the halcyon days of great landed estates. In early March 1940, subdividers acquired three of the town's grander properties. *Newmar,* the 20-acre George A. Newhall estate, sold to Louis Lengfeld, *El Cerrito,* one-time home of Eugene de Sabla and later Jean de St. Cyr, was purchased by developer David D. Bohannon and C. Templeton Crocker's 118-acre *Uplands* went to W.O. Lang. In 1946 Tomlinson (Tim) Moseley purchased the 550-acre *Carolands*. Only Ralston Avenue was paved up the hill. Moseley covered the ground on horseback, laying out streets. One night, after dinner in the big house, Moseley's family lingered around the table to come up with 50 names for streets in the *Carolands Tract*. Thus, for example, there was *Barbara, Denise, Robin, Robinwood, Darrell, Craig, Alberta* — all named for members of the Moseley family, relatives or friends. In 1912 the Carolans planted the bald hill with a forest of 20,000 trees. Moseley's bulldozers knocked thousands of them down. Pushed into a massive pile and set aflame, the eucalyptus burned for two years.

Eucalyptus Hill Farm

Dorothy Barrett purchased 72 acres (on lower Tournament Drive) from Celia Tobin Clark for $255,000 in 1947. The acquisition, including three brick homes and a luxurious 19-stall stable (designed by Chicago architect David Adler, 1928), became *Eucalyptus Hill Farm,* Hillsborough's last thoroughbred breeding ranch. Barrett raised three to four horses per year, several of which became champions, until the ranch was condemned in the late 1950s to make way for construction of Aragon High School on a San Mateo section of the property. *"We were pretty far out in the country back then,"* recalls Mrs. Barrett, *"we had a fire out there once and the fire department couldn't find us."* Closure of *Eucalyptus Hill Farm* signaled an end to a local equestrian tradition begun in 1875 when wealthy coffee merchant William Corbitt established *San Mateo Stock Farm* east of the tracks in Burlingame (that property was later purchased by Francis Carolan, who called it *Crossways Farm*).

Fashion show at *Uplands*

The day of the grand mansion with dozens of acres of undulating lawn and finely manicured gardens had passed by the 1950s, and great estates began to give way to subdivision. Where manorial houses remained, some were used for other purposes. *Uplands* became a private high school (for girls only), and in the early '70s W.W. Crocker's once regal *Sky Farm* (rebuilt in the 1930s) suffered the same fate (though co-educational). *Rosecourt,* the *White House, Strawberry Hill, La Dolphine* and the *Uplands* were regularly sought for charity functions, fashion shows and other fundraising events. During the '70s the Ford Foundation offered to spend $3.5 million on a Center for Advanced Study in Behavioral Science to be established at *Home Place,* one-time home of Jennie Crocker Henderson. The town council blocked the proposal. Countess Lillian Dandini, mistress of the *Carolands* who died in 1975, willed her Black Mountain chateau to the town for use as a cultural center or library. Such building utilization would have required amending Hillsborough's charter. Fearing this change could set a precedent and alter the residential character of the town, it was defeated by voters.

V.M. Molotov shaking hands with Helen Cameron, 1945

At the conclusion of World War II in 1945, the Soviets became thoroughly enchanted with the splendor of Hillsborough when hard-faced Soviet Foreign Minister Andrei Gromyko closeted himself in the Spreckels mansion for the kick-off of the United Nations. So taken was he with the *bourgeois* atmosphere of the Peninsula, he returned in 1951 for the signing of the peace treaty with Japan, this time barricading himself in the fortress-like magnificence of C. Templeton Crocker's *Uplands*, paying $250 a day for the privilege. In 1955, for a gathering of the United Nations in San Francisco, Soviet Prime Minister Vyacheslav M. Molotov and 35 KGB guards took over the Neal McNeil home on Willow Road. French Foreign Minister Antoine Pinay, British Foreign Secretary Harold Macmillan and Secretary of State John Foster Dulles all made their way down the Bayshore to sip wine and vodka while nibbling caviar on toast on Hillsborough's capitalist soil. They left with pockets full of Russian cigarettes, which Molotov handed out as mementos of the occasion. Molotov is pictured shaking hands with Helen Cameron in 1945.

Crystal Springs School

While critics disagree on the architectural distinction of *Uplands*, designed in 1912 by architect Willis Polk for C. Templeton Crocker, the mansion, which allegedly cost $1.5 million (including landscaping) and presently houses Crystal Springs Uplands School, has become a Peninsula landmark. The original house, with 35,000 square feet of living space, contained 39 rooms including 12 bedrooms and 12 baths. During Cold War "bomb drills" in the 1950s, when nuclear attack was anticipated, South Hillsborough School children were marched to nearby *Uplands* and sheltered in the 10,000 square foot basement, considered impregnable to any bomb. (West School children sought safety in a basement closet of *Carolands* while those from North School took cover in Jennie Henderson's *Home Place.*)

During the 1950s the old home became the Crystal Springs School, a private lyceum for girls. Seldom have students found themselves in more palatial surroundings. Here June Eastman, Ellen Kauffman and Christian Bosschart do homework in the school's ornate library. The institution became *Crystal Springs Uplands* and went co-educational in 1977.

Library at Crystal Springs School, circa 1955

Countess Lillian Virginia Remillard Dandini photographed on the grand staircase of *Chateau Remillard*

Lillian Virginia Remillard Dandini, daughter of Oakland, California, brickmaker Peter Nicholas Remillard, saved the 96-room *Chateau Carolands* from almost certain destruction when she purchased it and three acres of land for $80,000 in 1950. She called the home *Chateau Remillard*. A patron of arts and music, she frequently opened the house to grand functions. In 1961, presidential press secretary Pierre Salinger is alleged to have brought President John Kennedy's request that the four-story, French-renaissance chateau become his Western White House. "No possibility," the feisty Dandini informed the president. The same answer was allegedly sent to Bing and Kathryn Crosby who wanted to buy the house.

At age 50, in 1932, Lillian Remillard married Alessandro Olioli Dandini, a handsome Mexican-born Italian count. She was delighted to become a countess. Although they lived together fewer than six years and were finally divorced in 1946, she never relinquished the noble title. In 1965, Countess Dandini was named Hillsborough's *Citizen of the Year*, the first person to be so honored. She died in 1973 at age 93.

Helen Cameron (center) with the Duke and Duchess of Windsor

"You must believe me when I tell you that I have found it impossible . . . to discharge my duty as king as I would wish to do without the help and support of the woman I love."

Friday, Dec. 11, 1936. The radio broadcast of England's king, Edward VIII, announcing his abdication in order to marry American divorcée Wallis Warfield Simpson. His brother, George VI, gave him the title Duke of Windsor. He and Mrs. Simpson were married in June 1937.

In 1959, while on international tour, the duke and duchess visited Hillsborough as guests of Helen Cameron, where they were photographed with their hostess at *Rosecourt*. They are also shown relaxing with their omnipresent pet pugs.

Duke and Duchess of Windsor

Christian de Guigné

Christian de Guigné III was 18 in 1927 when his 38-year old father, an American Army World War I veteran and popular Hillsborough poloist, died. Young de Guigné III inherited substantial estates, held in trust until his 30th birthday, with Wells Fargo Bank and grandfather Christian de Guigné Sr. acting as trustees. *(Christian de Guigné Sr., a French count (born 1846) who became part of the Peninsula aristocracy by marrying Mary Katharine Parrott (1879), lived until 1942 at Chateau Senejac, the ancestral family estate in the Champagne region of France outside Bordeaux.)*

De Guigné III became master of magnificent *Guignicourt*, a home set amid 47 rustic Hillsborough acres adjacent to Crystal Springs Road. The French styled hilltop estate had been constructed by his father (1913). The family owned Stauffer Chemical Company. Christian III and wife Eleanor (née Christenson) posed for a photograph, seated poolside with son Christian IV (April 1961). The family, with second son Charles (right) is also shown. Christian III died in 1979. Christian IV acquired the Hillsborough property; Charles took over Chateau Senejac.

Christian de Guigné III with family at *Guignicourt*

105

Mr. & Mrs. William Willard Crocker

During the 1920s banker William Willard Crocker (son of William H. Crocker) and his family moved to *Sky Farm*. Built in the '90s, the wood-framed home near Skyline Boulevard burned in one of the town's more spectacular blazes (1928). *"Build me a palace,"* was Crocker's order to architect Arthur Brown Jr. The result was an immense, 53-room structure of reinforced concrete with indoor swimming grotto, squash court and spacious wine cellar built inside a vault. The grand house served as a gallery for Crocker's famed art collection. Built in a wooded, 500-acre forest, the place was known for spectacular landscaping and showy flower gardens. Crocker even maintained an apple orchard *exclusively for the deer*. A dozen resident servants and a daily staff of 24 were required for smooth operation. The master of *Sky Farm* always kept 14-16 cows so that the estate could be assessed as a farm. In 1971 the mansion became *Nueva Day School*, an elite private lyceum established four years before in Menlo Park. Crocker is pictured during the 1960s with his third wife, the former Elizabeth Fullerton Coleman. After his death she became a duchess by marriage to the Duke of Manchester.

W.W. Crocker's *Sky Farm*

Charles Clegg & Lucius Beebe

LUCIUS BEEBE SETS A STYLE

JANUARY 16, 1939 10 CENTS

"All I want is the best of everything . . ." bon-vivant, raconteur, gourmet and dandy Lucius Beebe once wrote. And he usually got it. In 1963, after a successful career as newspaper columnist, publisher and nostalgist, during which he'd frequently referred to *"nutty California,"* a place he likened to an *"over-crowded asylum run by inmates,"* Beebe and collaborator Charles Clegg established a winter residence on Vista Road in Hillsborough. Clegg told reporters he wasn't certain how many rooms the place had but that there were five bathrooms. Beebe became a local personality for his weekly "explosion of brimstone" in the *Chronicle.* Forever a sarcastic curmudgeon, Beebe frequently wrote about the town's "perfumed" society, where the kids play Robin Hood like all other youngsters, except in Hillsborough they *"steal from the poor and give to the rich."* Beebe and Clegg were expert storytellers of the American West, especially the saga of the railroads. Their tales found their way into virtually every periodical of note. Beebe wrote 35 books, many co-authored by Clegg. *Luscious Lucius,* as Walter Winchell called him, died of a heart attack at the Vista Road house in 1966. Companion Clegg died at the same elegant home in 1979.

The Crosby house between Jackling and Armsby drives

Singer-entertainer Bing Crosby and wife Kathryn moved into this luxurious French-style North Hillsborough home in 1964. The original owner (1929) had been Lindsay Howard of the Howard Buick Co. Subsequently it was purchased by Lindsay's father, Charles Howard, well known for his ownership of *Seabiscuit*, phenomenal racehorse of the 1930s. The Crosbys, initially uneasy in Hillsborough society, eventually became members of the country club and comfortably settled in. When their children attended local schools, Kathy Crosby frequently worked as a substitute teacher. For several years the Crosbys filmed Minute Maid orange juice commercials, for Christmas airing, at the home.

The Crosbys were well known for their *genuine* English butler, who had once worked for Queen Elizabeth II while she was still a princess. Alan Fisher watched over the house, advised the family on social etiquette and warded off unnecessary intrusions. Following the singer's death, Fisher returned to England. In 1982 he was hired to serve Prince Charles and Princess Diana at Kensington Palace. Fisher admitted that while he got along well with the Crosby family, he never thought much of Bing's singing or acting.

Bing and Kathryn Crosby

The Arthur Dale King home in the late 1920s

One of the least known architectural treasures of the community is the estate at 835 Chiltern Road built during the late 1920s by lumber and oil millionaire Arthur Dale King. Three houses were erected on the lushly landscaped six-acre property. In addition to the English-style main dwelling, others were for daughters, Geraldine (Mrs. Winston Stuart Cowgill) and Dale Florence (Mrs. Charles Christenson de Bonchamps). The house with many chimneys (most of which were purely for decoration) was renowned for intricately detailed moldings, parquet floors and leaded glass windows. Large bedroom suites on the second floor offered stunning views of San Francisco Bay. Arthur King, who dropped out of school at 13, always said his fortune was more luck than anything else. Of English and Scots heritage, he was extremely thrifty, insisting on saving string, creating large balls for reuse. He drove old and unimpressive cars and refused to pay a person to clean his swimming pool, preferring to do so himself. He traveled extensively and became knowledgeable in architecture and furniture design. His home reflected the distinctive styles of the Cotswold and Chiltern hills in England. King was responsible for naming Chiltern Road in Hillsborough.

Newhall Manor, **designed by A. Page Brown, was built in 1892**

Perhaps no 20th century Hillsborough personality was more politically prominent than Caspar Weinberger. He served in the California legislature (1952–1958), was U.S. Secretary of Health, Education and Welfare (1973–1975) and U.S. Secretary of Defense (1981–1988). In other activities, he wrote book reviews and columns for the San Francisco *Chronicle* (1958–1968) and was moderator of a weekly television show during the same period. He was a vice president and director of the Bechtel Group of Companies (1975–1981). All of this is in addition to several directorships and service on a variety of other government commissions. The Weinbergers, members of the Burlingame Club, lived in *Newhall Manor* and at a home in Forest View Avenue. Among the *Newhall Manor* residents were George A. Newhall and Howard Spreckels. It was lived in by the Weinbergers from 1975–1982.

Jane and Cap Weinberger

Luciano and Mrs. Pavarotti, Kurt Herbert Adler and Ada Regan

Grandissimo Pavarotti . . . More than 500 heard Luciano Pavarotti sing, Sept 23, 1979. This was the Italian tenor's first Bay Area recital, a benefit for the San Francisco Opera Association, staged in the sprawling formal gardens of Mr. and Mrs. Barrie F. Regan's 50-acre *Strawberry Hill.* Originally called *Villa Rose*, the Italian-renaissance house and gardens, designed and built by San Francisco architect Lewis P. Hobart (1912) for financier-industrialist Joseph D. Grant and later owned by Charles Blyth, was acquired by the Regans in 1975 for $1,150,000. Of Hills-borough's original great estates, *Strawberry Hill is* the largest not subdivided by developers. The tuxedoed Pavarotti arrived 30 minutes late, white handkerchief in one hand and a diet cola in the other. Guests sipped wine during the intermission. The memorable two-hour program, including arias and songs by Verdi, Bizet, Liszt and Schubert, concluded with encores and bravos. Pavarotti, a personal friend of Barrie and Ada Regan, *Strawberry Hill's* Italian owners, returned in 1983 to star in the Metro-Goldwyn-Mayer film *Yes, Giorgio,* featuring the house and gardens. Pictured are Pavarotti, his wife, Kurt Herbert Adler (director of the San Francisco Opera Co.) and Ada Regan.

Chief William Key, 1990

Hillsborough's large estates and wooded terrain have combined to make the canine corps (established 1959) an essential part of the police department. The dogs are trained in search, rescue and attack. Pictured, taking part in a missing persons investigation (1971) near Crocker Lake, are Officers Tom Musser (with Kilo) and Jack Fena (with Takara). Also shown is William Key, who joined the Hillsborough force in 1957 and served as chief from 1976–1990.

Tom Musser and Jack Fena

Helen Wills ultimately won eight Wimbledon titles

Tennis competition awakened in Hillsborough hearts after the turn of the century. There was much excitement when Jennie Crocker married U.S. Davis Cup champion Malcolm Douglas Whitman (1912). Their sister-in-law, Helene Irwin Crocker, soon began organizing a women's league.

Competition reached a fever pitch in May 1926, when 1,500 gathered at the Burlingame Club to watch the women square off against the men. Bets were placed. Helen Wills Moody and young Helen Crocker faced club champions Lawrence McCreery and William Leib. Moody-Crocker took the first set, the men the second, and the finale went to the women. Clubmen, who almost universally had bet on the men, paid off—in $100 bills.

Danvers House, **erected during the early 1920s**

Paul Irving Fagan

Thirty-room *Danvers House*, designed by architect Arthur Brown Jr. and built in 1922 for San Francisco financier William Clarkson Van Antwerp, originally occupied 16 acres near Jackling Drive. Access was via a long, winding driveway past a small lake and grand sweeps of lawn punctuated with ancient oaks. The house is celebrated for unique architectural features and genuine Old World ambiance. Even floor boards were taken from the *Duchess of Kent*, an English sailing vessel which had been slated for destruction. Throughout, intricate woodwork is hand-carved and delicately-paned leaded glass windows are hand-set. The enormous marble fireplace in the 38-foot high Great Hall was brought from the home of Britain's Puritan leader Oliver Cromwell who had ruled England as Lord Protector during the 1650s. In the late 1920s, *Danvers House* sold to importer-exporter Paul I. Fagan and his wife Helene, the former Helene Irwin Crocker. Fagan became a director of Pacific Transport Lines operating freighters throughout the Pacific and a director of Pioneer Kettleman Oil. Later, he acquired ownership of the *Seals*, a San Francisco baseball team.

The White House, **1986**

William H. Howard, son of pioneer settler W.D.M. Howard, built a 36-room, brown-shingled chalet on the south side of San Mateo Creek during the 1870s. He called it *Uplands*. After his death the house was acquired by the Crocker family. C. Templeton Crocker later rechristened it *Montes Robles*. He despised the house, which he sold in 1915 with the stipulation the new owner move it without harming the trees. Relocation to the opposite side of the creek required use of 200 eight inch rollers drawn by mules. Rough terrain necessitated raising the structure as much as 50 feet off the ground. A 20-foot trestle was constructed for crossing the creek. In two months 18 men moved it 350 yards to *401 El Cerrito Avenue*. Ironically, in 1922 it was destroyed by fire. In 1930 owner George Hearst, son of the newspaper czar, retained architect Julia Morgan to rebuild along different lines; it became known as Hillsborough's *White House.*

In 1986 the house was completely reno-vated and opened as a Decorators' Show House by the Coyote Point Museum Auxiliary. Formed in 1953, the auxiliary is an organization devoted to environmental education at the museum. It pioneered the concept of show houses as legitimate fund raising activities. Since its first house opening (1957), the organization has raised millions for the Coyote Point Museum.

Dita Wilbur and Sister Ida Martini, 1991

Susan Soto-Hall Phillips and Jan Anderton, circa 1950

Hillsborough residents support a myriad of Northern California charitable organizations, with emphasis on schools, environmental causes, medical research and the fine arts. High on the community's list of favorite causes is the Medical Mission Sisters, an international religious community of women who serve the sick in 25 countries. For more than a generation, fashion shows staged for the benefit of Medical Missions, usually in the garden of one of the great estates, have highlighted the late summer social scene. In 1991 Matilda (Dita) Wilbur, *grande dame* of Hillsborough society and benefactor of the organization, was honored with roses on her 91st birthday. She is pictured here receiving congratulations from Sister Ida Martini. Hillsborough women have also been especially supportive of the Children's Hospital at Stanford Auxiliary. They operate the Garden Cafe, a lunchroom in Burlingame, with profits going to the hospital. Susan Soto-Hall Phillips and Jane Anderton are shown, circa 1950, at one of the many fundraising events for the Children's Hospital Auxiliary.

William and Katherine Boyd with President George Bush

Katherine Boyd and California Gov. George Deukmejian

Traffic was a nightmare along the Peninsula, Oct. 29, 1990, when President George Bush went to breakfast in Hillsborough at the Bridge Road home of Mr. and Mrs. William Sprott Boyd, longtime Bush boosters. Breakfast was preceded by champagne and a 45 minute "mix and mingle" in the Boyd parlor before the president and 75 invited guests retired to a large tent erected on the lawn for the meal. Bush devotees from all over the West attended, paying $25,000 a person for the privilege. Debonair William Boyd assures that we "served a good English breakfast," including cantaloupe, eggs, sausage, bacon and lamb chops, all catered by the St. Francis Hotel. Everybody got pictures snapped with the president. Bush spoke for 20 minutes. The party raised more than $750,000 for the California Republican party. Perhaps that accounts for the smiles of both Bush and California Gov. George Deukmejian. With the president are William Boyd and his wife Katherine.

The MacFarlane children welcoming President Clinton

President Bill Clinton flanked by Thadarine and Victor MacFarlane at their Hillsborough home in March of 1996

The Democratic National Committee cleared more than $500,000, Saturday evening March 9, 1996, when President Bill Clinton dropped by for dinner at the Tournament Drive home of Victor and Thadarine MacFarlane. Mrs. MacFarlane, a native of New Orleans, planned a home town-type affair with a zydeco band and Cajun food. A special order of chicory coffee along with bags of fresh crayfish (sealed in their own fat) were brought from Louisiana. Hillsborough Police Chief Robert McNichols mobilized an 85-officer security force composed of personnel from the San Mateo County Sheriff's office, the California Highway Patrol and his own officers. The command post for the event was on the campus of nearby College of San Mateo. MacFarlane's Tournament Drive neighbors, most who claimed to belong to the opposition party, nevertheless generously opened their garages for the comfort of the 35-40 members of presidential press corps. The President, who gave a short speech and shook hands with the almost 200 guests, left after two hours — carting a doggy bag of gumbo.

In the 1890s, residents of this area found Hillsborough more of a frame of mind than a specific geographic area. Only later did it become an organized community. Through the years, although the town has changed dramatically, much of its original uniqueness has been maintained. The accompanying photograph shows three 10-year-olds planting a flowering plum tree at North Hillsborough School. Arbor Day has always been recognized as an annual event in the community. North School, on property formerly owned by William H. Crocker, occupied what had once been the Crocker swimming pool.

Stacey Sebanc, Allison Kiley and Matt Bosschart at North Hillsborough School in 1983

Acknowledgments

The following depositories and organizations provided photographs for use in this book:

Burlingame Historical Society
Coyote Point Museum Auxillary
Crystal Springs Uplands School
Doerr Photography (Burlingame)
Grace Cathedral Archives
Hillsborough City School District
Hillsborough Town Hall
Hillsborough Police Department
Thomas John Gibbons Photography
Pacific Bell Archives
San Francisco History Center (San Francisco Public Library)
San Francisco *Chronicle*
San Mateo County Historical Museum
San Mateo *Times*
Save-the-Redwoods League

Families or individuals, some now deceased, who contributed photographs:
Vincent Asai, Dorothy Barrett, William S. Boyd, Florence (Welch) Bruce, Nessie Chesebrough, Barbara Coghlan, James Davies, Alexandre Charles de Limur, Benjamin and Barbara Lee Follett, Phyllis (Koshland) Friedman, Alan Henderson, Robert Henderson, Lin and Jennifer Ho, Bert Horn, David Johnson, Grace Jones, William Key, Jacqueline Low, Thadarine MacFarlane, Elizabeth Mack, Consuelo (Nini) Martin, Cynthia McCormick, Robert Folger Miller, Gordon and Randi Murray, Robin Moseley O'Connell, Margaret O'Keefe, William Parrott, Harry Poett, Barrie and Ada Regan, Beth (Wisnom) Remington, Beverly Sebanc, Michael H. de Young Tobin, Francis Toldi, Laurette (Bona) Toldi, Dorothea Walker and Suzanne Crocker White. Others made family photographs available but did so on the promise of anonymity.

For their expertise and encouragement, the authors thank social historian and journalist Mary Jane Clinton-Zirkel; Mark Still, professor of history at College of San Mateo; Michael Lampen, archivist for Grace Cathedral; Marian Holmes, archivist for the San Mateo County Historical Museum; Sally Kibbee, San Francisco *Chronicle* photo historian; Marilyn Short and Martha Rossman of the Burlingame Historical Society; Jeanne Thivierge, local history specialist at the Redwood City Public Library; and Pat Akre, photo archivist of the San Francisco History Center, San Francisco Public Library.

A special debt of gratitude is offered to longtime Hillsborough resident Betty Horn, the town's *unofficial* historian who met frequently with the authors to assist in identifying photographs, make introductions and help arrange interviews. Some of the confused links with Hillsborough's past were successfuly identified and explained thanks to her unselfish assistance.

A successful pictorial history relies almost solely upon the quality of its photographic reproductions. Recognition is given to consultant Michael Russell of Lafayette, California, who was responsible for reproducing many priceless images, some more than a hundred years old. More than once he was asked to copy framed photographs sealed behind glass without first removing them from walls. For him, no photographic challenge was too great.

Bibliographic Notes

This is the first book-length survey of the Hillsborough community ever undertaken. In preparing it, we have relied on newspaper accounts and drawn from the *San Mateo Times*, the *News Leader*, the *Burlingame Advance-Star*, the *Burlingame-Hillsborough Boutique and Villager*, the *San Mateo County Times Gazette*, the *San Mateo County News* along with the *Redwood City Democrat* and the *Redwood City Tribune*. During the years before the Second World War, Hillsborough activities, social and otherwise, were faithfully reported by all San Francisco newspapers. We've paid particular attention to the society, business and sports sections of the San Francisco *Chronicle, Examiner, Call, Bulletin* and the *Daily Alta*.

For eyewitness glimpses of early personalities, William Heath Davis' book, *Seventy-five Years in California* (1967), should be consulted. Joseph D. Grant's memoir, *Redwoods and Reminiscences* (1973), contains an excellent look at Hillsborough's society during its early years. Davenport Bromfield's *The San Mateo We Knew* (1957) is a well-written firsthand account of life in San Mateo, Burlingame and Hillsborough after the 1890s. And, though it is available only in French, André Poniatowski's account of turn-of-the-century Burlingame in *D'un Siècle à L'Autre* (1934) is outstanding. This book gives the reader some of the complexity of Poniatowski's business relationship with William H. Crocker and the extent of their investments.

Secondary works worthy of mention include *The Town of Hills-borough Historic Building Survey* (1990), Mitchell Postel's *History of the Burlingame Country Club* (1982), David Warren Ryder's *Great Citizen: A Biography of William H. Crocker* (1962) and Barbara Donohoe Jostes' study of the Parrott family, *John Parrott, 1811-1884* (1972). For fun, readable and often controversial accounts, see Frances Moffet's *Dancing on the Brink of the World* (1977) and Julia C. Altrocchi's *Those Spectacular San Franciscans* (1949). Historical columns by Millie Robbins, published in the San Francisco *Chronicle* and the *San Mateo Times*, offer gossipy but accurate vignettes of Hillsborough society. We have also drawn from early editions of the *Argonaut*, the *Wave* (a periodical published at Del Monte), *Sunset Magazine* and the more scholarly *California Historical Society Quarterly*.

This book could not have been prepared without assistance and information from many present and former Hillsborough residents. Those who have been interviewed include: Dorothy Barrett, Andrew Berwick, William S. Boyd, Geoffrey Bromfield, Florence (Welch) Bruce, Nessie Chesebrough, Christian de Guigné IV, Phyllis (Koshland) Friedman, Benjamin Follett, Virginia Fuller, Barbara (Kahn) Gardner, Leonard Glover, Alan Henderson, Robert Henderson, Henry Howard, Jack and Betty Ken, William Key, Jacquelin Low, Robert McNichols, Thadarine MacFarlane, Elizabeth Mack, Patricia (Kahn) Margolis, Consuelo (Nini Tobin) Martin, Robert Folger Miller, Robin Moseley O'Connell, William Parrott, Barrie and Ada Regan, Ruth (Easton) Rogers, Fred Schwartz, Beverly Sebanc, Mariana (Casserly) Smith, Paul and Ruth Steiner, Michael H. de Young Tobin, Laurette Toldi, Dorothea Walker, James Waters, Suzanne Crocker White and David Wisnom.

Index

125

127